The History of Miss Melmoth. In two Volumes. By the Author of The Fine Lady. ... of 2

THE HISTORY OF MISS MELMOTH.

In TWO VOLUMES

VOL II

By the AUTHOR of the FINE LADY

" Let Emma's hapless case be falsely told,
" By the rash young, or the ill-natur'd old,
" Let every tongue in various censures chuse,
" Acquit with coldness, or with spite accuse
" Fair Truth at last her radiant head shall raise,
" And malice vanquish'd heighten Virtue's praise

PRIOR's Henry and Emma

DUBLIN

PRINTED FOR JAMES WILLIAMS, AT No 5,
SKINNER-ROW MDCCLXXII

THE HISTORY OF MISS MELMOTH.

LETTER LI

To Miſs VERL

Groſvenor-Square, Auguſt 19

I AM exceſſively concerned to hear of the imprudent choice your father has made for your mother-in-law But indeed, my dear Sidney, I wiſh you would a little reflect on what you have written to me I am perſuaded, had you taken a copy, or had only given your letter a ſecond peruſal, you would never have ſent it. I can make ſome allowances for the firſt effuſions of a heart like yours But conſider, my love, in how near a relation the perſon ſtands, whom you treat with ſo little reſpect —I really am amazed at his moderation

Parents have an undoubted right to diſpoſe of themſelves without the concurrence or conſent of their children.—We have often ſeen children invade the authority of parents, and diſpoſe of themſelves againſt the conſent, or without the approbation of their parents.

You always ſuppoſed Sir William would marry; it is true, you have not much reaſon to be pleaſed. Miſs Arnold wants delicacy, if ſhe is not deficient in other reſpects, which for your ſake, I ſincerely hope ſhe may not; ſince, whatever indiſcretions the world might adjudge to Miſs Arnold, would extremely hurt you to be recogniſed in Lady Vere. It would be a reflection on my Sidney.—Did ſhe not introduce her into the houſe? will be aſked.

I own, on a candid retroſpect of the lady's behaviour all along, ſhe never thoroughly pleaſed me. You was ſo partial to her, that I was unwilling to appear incredulous. I make no doubt ſhe was unfortunate. Perhaps—and moſt likely betrayed into vice. Yet view her diſpaſſionately; did ſhe retain that ſoft languor—that dejection of ſpirits—that modeſt, diffident humility that firſt charmed you?——I believe you will anſwer, ſhe did not.

Do you remember, I am ſure I do perfectly—and was ſhocked, becauſe it convinced me ſhe was not the pure innocent ſhe at firſt affected to be thought—you was one day reading a novel, and coming to a part where the heroine of the piece was in great danger, from an attempt on her honor by one on whom ſhe relied; upon a light ſpeech of the betrayer, Miſs Arnold burſt out in a violent fit of laughter. I took an invincible prejudice againſt her from that moment, tho' I never revealed it to any one.

I repeat, ſhe may have been ſurpriſed into vice; but I can never believe from her ſubſequent behaviour, ſhe did not conſent to continue ſome time at leaſt with her ſeducer.

She

She is to the laſt degree ungrateful to you—and has acted a very indelicate part by your Father. —She is now his Wife—Moſt likely he will find uneaſineſs enough from matrimony, without any addition from you—Your making him unhappy cannot diſſolve the marriage-vow, but may, as he ſays, alienate the ſhare you have at preſent in his affections. He thinks he has injured you—and will ſeek to repay by kindneſs that injuſtice. To a girl of your ſpirit, no doubt it is diſagreeable to have a mother-in-law ſet over you—and ſuch a one too, as will aſſume to herſelf all the arrogance of a ſtep-dame.

But however, you muſt ſubmit to your father: carrying things with ſo high a hand will not avail.

The Darnley family are arrived—They came to town late laſt night—Sir George ſent a general compliment to us, importing he would wait on us this morning—I hear his rap—You will excuſe my ſhort epiſtle—Adieu.

CAROLINE MELMOTH.

LETTER LII.

To Miſs MELMOTH.

Vere-Park, Auguſt, 21.

I Thank my deareſt Caroline for her counſel, and will endeavour to profit by it.

I believe I treated my father with too much *hauteur*, and will alter my carriage to him. But as for her *ladyſhip*, I am more and more provoked with her, fawning and imperious by turns, as ſhe ſees occaſion. Nay, the other day ſhe ſaid to me,

"Miſs Vere, your ſervant treats me with diſre-
"ſpect. You will oblige me by parting with
"him."

"Have you any more old acquaintance then to
"introduce?"

"No, my dear, nor do I very well know what
"you mean. But you ſhould chooſe yourſelf
"whom you pleaſed ſhould attend you."

"I thank you much, Madam," affectedly
courteſying, "for the permiſſion you allow me.
"But it is ſufficient for you to be familiar with
"your own ſervant, and leave mine to his own
"buſineſs."

"My dear Sidney, I would be your friend, if
"you would ſuffer me. I have ſome influence o-
"ver your father, as you may perceive; but be-
"lieve me, I will never uſe it to your diſadvan-
"tage, while you behave to me with civility and
"reſpect."

I had juſt then read your letter; nor can I give
you a ſtronger proof of the efficacy of your advice,
than in informing you, I did not fly at her ladyſhip's head-dreſs immediately.

But not a word more, only to tell you how im-
menſely I have been duped by the artful creature.
She ſhewed my promiſſory note to my father,
which ſo piqued him, as it tended to rob him of
his fair one, that he ordered his ſteward to deduct
fifteen Pounds a quarter from my ſtipend. I am
not a very extravagant girl, ſo I do not much
mind. However, I will never take the leaſt notice of it to my father, even if he was to ſtop my
allowance quite; if he can be mean enough to diſtreſs his daughter in pecuniary affairs, ſhe has
much too great a ſhare of pride to complain.

Your account of Lord L's inſolence is amaz-
ing, but not unlike him, as I have heard. His re-
formation, if ſincere, may ſave a great many from
deſtruction

destruction I was told he had engaged in several fine exploits—for which he richly deserved the gallows, but that he had the precaution to use a feigned name Vile creature! I did not think, my love, you had so much spirit; but it was the spirit of virtue

I congratulate you, my dear, on the arrival of your Darnley say something civil to him for me. —I love him for your sake; and am

Yours,

SIDNEY VERE.

LETTER LIII

To Miss VERE

Grosvenor-Square, August 25

MISS Grafton and I have had a little altercation, occasioned by the impertinence of her behaviour I was, since dinner, answering a letter I had just received from the dear Darnley

Somehow or other, Sidney, he has engaged me in a correspondence, but of that anon

Miss Grafton abruptly entered my closet I huddled up his letter, and laid my own aside "What "are you doing, Caroline?"

"Writing"

"What?"

"A Letter"

"To Whom?"

"A Friend"

"I must see what you are about"

"I Tell you, I am writing"

"Aye but I must see to whom"

"You must!" turning and fixing my eyes upon her, with a moderate degree of contemptuous surprise in my countenance.

"You must first obtain my leave."

"Positively, Caroline, I must, and will see to whom you are writing."

"When you can convince me you have any right to talk thus to me, I may think it worth my while to contend with you. But with all submission to Miss Grafton, I suppose this closet and its contents sacred to me, nor liable to the infringement of arbitrary Power: general-Warrants you know," smiling, "are of no force now."

She reddened. "The niece of a man, Miss Melmoth, who rescued you from starving, might be intitled, I should have thought, to a better behaviour from you."

"The uncle of that niece," returned I, with scorn, "would have blushed to have made such a recrimination. But you should remember, by law, you had as little right to the bounty of my honored benefactor, as the little wretch rescued from starving.

"The grateful remembrance of what I owe the best of men, I endeavour to repay the best of women: to them my obligations are unequalled; but I must likewise say to Miss Grafton, I can at least return her, with interest, all I owe her, and that chiefly by being silent."

"Your birth is conspicuous in your very polite treatment of me."

"The obscurity of my birth, Miss Grafton, has never yet given rise to any action for which I need blush."

"Blush! no, I believe not. Some people are incapable of blushing," with a sneer.

"It

"It muſt be thoſe then, whoſe crimes have rendered them callous to all ſhame But detection will make moſt people bluſh, tho' the ſhortneſs of their memories makes them forget the occaſion" I threw my eyes upon her in ſuch a manner, as made it impoſſible for her to miſtake my meaning, ſhe did not She bit her lip, and and looked much as I had ſeen her once before, however, recovering herſelf, "So you poſitively will not let me ſee what you have written."

"I do not chooſe it."

"How can you be ſo ill-natured?"

"It is rather a proof of my good-nature, as I believe the contents would afford you little pleaſure

"I wiſh I could ſee all you write to Miſs Vere"

"You would not have patience to read it"

"Why not?"

"Becauſe I write every incident that occurs And the reading ſome things, would not afford you ſo much ſatisfaction perhaps, as the reality might."

"I profeſs, I do not underſtand you"

"As Oſmyn ſays, I would not have thee"

"Well, well, but you ſhall not turn me from my purpoſe you muſt make me your confidante" And approached to take up the letter—I ſnatched it from her, with anger "What inſolence is this! By what right do you invade my privacy? Such behaviour is both unbecoming you to offer, and my putting up with"

My ſpeech brought an anſwer, which occaſioned a ſmart reply, ſhe returned it full of acrimony, I rejoined · and we downright ſcolded Did you think I could ſcold, Sidney? Out-did you all to nothing! After this ſmart conteſt, I remained miſtreſs of the field.

Upon reflection, I am ſorry, but ſhe urged me by her low invectives on the myſtery of my birth, —to ſay things in anſwer, which I had promiſed myſelf ſhould be buried in total oblivion.

After tea, I ſought an opportunity of ſpeaking to Miſs Grafton—you know I cannot bear any-one ſhould have reaſon to be reſentful to me. I told her "I was extremely ſorry I had ſuffered paſſion "to get the better of reaſon and politeneſs; but "hoped ſhe would excuſe it."—She ſaid, She had "likewiſe been very wrong, and begged I would "not think any further about it; but that we "might mutually forgive each other."—So peace is proclaimed once more.

I hate nothing worſe than theſe quarrels. They greatly leſſen the bands of friendſhip. It is true, Miſs Grafton and I were never very cordial friends, but I hope I ſhall be able to keep well with her.

I condemn myſelf more than any one would—herſelf excepted, for giving into a clandeſtine correſpondence with Sir George. I was determined to remain ſatisfied with the proofs I had already received of his affection, without accepting any illicit ones. But our prudent reſolves appear weak, when oppoſed to the rhetoric of a pleading lover.

He obtained my permiſſion to write to me. The means he undertook to render practicable. I declare, I knew not his method, 'till Jenny the next day preſented me a letter. I was ſorry he had choſe this means. It is laying ourſelves under the laſh of ſervants,—an evil we ought to guard againſt.

They are mercenary—and guided by one motive,—intereſt. Jenny has not, I believe, any reaſon to complain of either of her employers: Yet, I do aſſure you, ſhe already claims a degree of familiarity,—tho' I never treated her with haughtineſs,—bordering upon impertinence, from the conſequence ſhe thinks ſhe is of to us.

It

It was but yesterday I reproved her, with neglecting some directions I had given her, when she told me, she thought I had too much reason to be pleased with her diligence, to accuse her of negligence Thus you see the inconvenience is very obvious, and the entering into any clandestine measure, productive of disagreeable consequences

I wish to extricate myself from a situation so painful to an ingenuous mind Mine, 'till I knew Sir George Darnley, knew not deceit Ah! why should a sentiment, so noble as that of true love, give birth to insincerity?

But then an open avowal of our attachment would most likely be productive of the—to us—dreadfullest misfortune

I have often asked my heart, are there any reasonable hopes of our gaining the approbation and participation of those, whose consent is absolutely necessary to effect an union?—My reason answers, there is not What then are we pursuing? A shadow—Courting our destruction But then my heart whispers me, I am ardently beloved by the most amiable of men Ah, my Sidney! there is so exquisite a pleasure in knowing one's-self the object of a tender passion, inspired too in the breast of the most lovely of men—on whom our eyes dwell with delight, and our heart approves,—to hear him repeat the dear sounds, to know he lives but for you—Away ye dull reasoners—your pleadings are vain Darnley, the dear, the faithful Darnley, loves me—He will be mine at least, the happiness I taste, when he tells me he will, would recompense an eternity of pain But I here will finish my rhapsody, with assuring you I am equally your devoted

CAROLINE MELMOTH.

P. S I am very glad to hear you profited so well by

by my letter of advice I am sure you are better pleased with yourself upon the occasion Never let persons you do not love have any plea against you, lest they should take advantage of it Adieu

---

LETTER LIV

To Miss VERE

Grosvenor-Square, Sept 4

I Have just escaped a most imminent danger, a plot of Miss Grafton's, I still think, notwithstanding her strong asseverations to the contrary Yet what end it could answer, I know not, even if it had not proved abortive Thanks be to Heaven, it did! I tremble on the recollection, Sidney! I might by this time have been the verest wretch existing

I will make you acquainted with the particulars without further preface

This afternoon, Mrs Grafton being out, Miss Grafton—who has been most amazingly civil since our closet-dialogue,—proposed our taking a walk You know it is an exercise I am fond of, tho' I can seldom partake of that pleasure in town.

We sallied out, John with us When we had gone some way, Miss Grafton recollected a message, which her aunt had desired her to deliver, of some consequence "I am vastly uneasy and "vext at my negligence," said she. "What shall "I do, Caroline?"

"If the delay will be attended with any incon-"venience, we had better return."

"No,"

"No," ſhe replyed, "I do not like to loſe "our *promenade* But if you will, we will ſend "John back, he will be infinitely more expediti-"ous than we, and there can be no danger in our "walking further without him"—I acquieſced John was ſent back upon his embaſſy, and we proceeded In a little time, Miſs Grafton aſked me, if I had ever walked in the Muſeum-Gardens? I anſwered, No—"Then," ſaid ſhe, "we will go "thither it is not far, nor can it fatigue us"

I knew not my way in that part of the town, having never been there but now-and-then, to pay a viſit in a coach I mentioned my ignorance, "O, be under no concern," ſaid Miſs Grafton, I "have been there many times, and am at no loſs "at all"

We chatted away on indifferent things very pleaſantly She was in perfect good-humour, and I ſecretly condemned myſelf, for making ſuch ſharp recriminations as I did ſome time ago

Juſt as we had got into the ſtreet, in which the gate of the garden is, we were accoſted by two ſmart-looking men, they were officers both One in his uniform, expreſſed great joy at ſeeing Miſs Grafton, and aſked after her friends She ſeemed no leſs pleaſed at the *rencontre* I had often heard her mention a young officer, with whom ſhe was acquainted at Coventry-races I naturally imagined this to be him, as ſhe always mentioned him with warmth.

He aſked her where ſhe was rambling, ſhe told him of our intention He begged to be permitted to attend us, to which ſhe made no objection: ſhe was wholly engroſſed by his converſation; which gave the other gentleman an opportunity of addreſſing himſelf to me.

We took ſeveral turns in the garden, and I hinted to Miſs Grafton it grew late She agreed readily

readily to go.—The gentlemen said, they could propose a nearer and pleasanter way than that we had taken before, which they observed was dusty and disagreeable, being chiefly thro' streets.

Miss Grafton consented, laughingly, to be guided by them, saying, "We have inlisted under your "banners, and have no inclination to desert."

We proceeded, Miss Grafton and the red-coat-man walking first, and the other, who was mighty assiduous, following with me. We went a back way, and arrived at another garden, the door of which stood open; it was, as Captain Campbell said, a thorough-fair. As we were going through, Miss Grafton suddenly caught hold of my arm, exclaiming, "Good God! what ails me? Support "me, or I shall fall." We all offered her our assistance immediately. She complained of a violent pain in her head, accompanied with a giddiness.

Captain Campbell begged she would walk into the house, and consent to take some remedy. She made some objections, which I thought, in such an exigence, altogether absurd; and I joined my intreaties that she would be persuaded.—She at length consented, and into the house we went. A maid-servant appeared, and brought her some hartshorn drops with water. She drank of it, and desired to go into the air, thinking she should be much better.

I prepared to attend her, really frightened at her indisposition; but she prevented me, saying, "she "would trouble the young woman further, and "would then make her a gratuity."

The two gentlemen remained with me in the parlour. In about a minute, Campbell left the room. I expressed some uneasiness at Miss Grafton's illness, at which the strange gentleman, I know not his name, smiled, and coming up to me, taking both my hands, said, looking stedfastly in my face, "It is a very lucky indisposition, since it has "left

" left me the opportunity of being alone with you."

I withdrew my hands at the beginning of this speech, which I thought sufficiently free. "You " have little compassion then, sir, for the sufferings " of your fellow creatures."—Very gravely.

" Of that sort, I have not much," returned he, smiling. " But Miss Grafton's having left us, is a " kind of reproach for losing so much time."

" I don't understand, sir."

" In the next room you will perhaps," replied he, opening a door, where as I stood I discovered a bed. " Come my charmer," continued he, approaching me, " in that room we may become " better acquainted."

" Your behaviour, sir," looking sternly at him, " seems to need an explanation, since——"

" Then thus I explain it, my angel," catching me in his arms, and kissing me.

Breaking from him, I exclaimed, " Insolent " monster! From whence proceed these indignities?"

" From your charms, my angel, since they " provoke me to reap the blessing offered me." and again approached me.

" Great Heaven! Am I to bear these insults? " Leave the room this instant."

" You command in a very pretty tone of voice " truly. But my lovely creature, you had better " lay aside your ranting airs, they may do with " some novice, who does not know the tricks of " ye all."

" Tricks! tricks! Gracious God! Who?— " What do you take me for?"

' Take you for! Why, notwithstanding the " killing frown with which you dress your lovely " face, I take you for a most charming, kind, " consenting fair one, who will in a few minutes " make me the happiest of mankind."

My eyes were now sufficiently opened. I threw myself

myself into a chair, and burst into a violent flood of tears. He drew near to me with an air of surprise, "For Heaven sake, my dear creature, why "these tears! Do you doubt my generosity and "honor?"

"O, by that last sacred word, sir," clasping my hands, "I adjure you to tell why, or for what "purpose, I was betrayed hither? But you need "not, my own heart sufficiently informs me "This is a deep-laid scheme indeed—Oh my "God! what will become of me!"

"You astonish me amazingly. Is it possible "I can be deceived!"

"O yes, O yes, as sure as I have been," sobbed I

"Are you not then one of those ladies who make "no scruple of meeting a man in one of these "genteel houses?"

"O no, Heaven forbid! No, sir, however ap- "pearances are against me, I am a woman of "strict honor and virtue. Indeed, indeed I am," lifting up my clasped hands, for I thought he looked as if he had rather not believe me. "I would "sooner forfeit my life than my pretensions to "either."

"Honor and virtue, madam, I revere where- "ever I find it."

"God for ever bless you! and forgive you all "your sins, for the comfort you have given me in "that assurance!"

"Amen, as I can acquit myself of any inten- "tional one here. But why did you come hither?"

"Innocently, as Heaven can witness. I knew "no more of the place or house than the infant "yet unborn. But I see the whole plan now. O "protect me, Heaven, from my cruel enemies!" And I redoubled my tears.

"Weep not, madam, you shall have no cause "from

"from me. And upon my knees I crave your "pardon for any freedom, the place, and your so "readily entering it, might induce me to take."

"I heartily forgive you, sir.—But for Heaven's "sake let me quit this horrid place; every thing "contributes to my terror."

"I shall ever think myself more than adequately "punished for my involuntary crime, by the re-"flection that my first interview, with a lady so "amiable as you appear, must lay a foundation for "an invincible prejudice—I see it by your looks."

"No, no, sir: see me safe out of this shocking "house, and I will promise ever to remember you "with gratitude. Heaven perhaps sent you to "protect me."

"That I will with my life. And as a proof of "my honorable intentions, I will neither request "your name nor place of abode. Tho' allow me "to say, your person I can never forget."

"Be so kind as to add to my obligations, sir, the "favor of procuring me a chair to carry me "home."

"Most readily, madam. And my next bu-"siness shall be, to oblige Campbell to unravel "this mysterious affair."

He left the room.

I instantly threw myself upon my knees, and poured forth my thanks to Heaven, for granting me thus signally its protection. I had not yet finished the effusions of my heart, when he entered again. I rose hastily.

"I can never pardon myself, madam," said he, "for the liberties I dared to offer you. But a "chair is at the door: permit me to make all the "reparation in my power, by placing you in it. "And may the God, you serve, ever protect you! "May I hope not to be remembred with hatred, "for I feel I shall then be most wretched."

By

By this time we had reached the door. No person appeared in my sight, a precaution which the gentleman used, that I might not be further distressed. I was just going to enter the chair, when I perceived Sir George Darnley's chariot drive slowly by; I ran back precipitately into the house, and almost involuntarily, so terrified I was. As soon as it had passed, I threw myself hastily into the chair; again thanked the gentleman; told the men to carry me to Bond-Street; and burst into a fresh flood of tears.

I was set down at the house of Mrs Jones, my Milliner; I bought a few trifles, and having discharged that chair, took another which brought me home.

I flew up to my chamber, and remained there lost in thought. Soon after Miss Grafton appeared. I felt my colour rise at sight of her. She began.

"I thank you Miss Melmoth, for your company."

"And I have the same obligation to you, Miss "Grafton; tho' thank Heaven, your diabolical "scheme did not take place."

"What do you mean?" with affected surprise.

"My meaning is pretty obvious." Disdainfully.

"I should have expected some apology, Miss "Caroline, for your leaving me, while I was in-"disposed, in the garden."

"I believe, Madam, you had company much "more agreeable to your inclination: but I assure "you, I will acquaint Mrs Grafton of the conse-quences of your plot, tho' the formation of it I cannot account for."

"You perplex me much with talking of a plot, "Miss Melmoth; but I *suppose you mean to* ex-"culpate yourself from the allegation I have laid "against you, of leaving me alone in a strange "place, and your parading away with two young "fellows equally unknown to you."

"Impotent

"Impotent insinuation! Can you affect this ignorance?—But it will not now serve your purpose, I give you my word I have sustained indignities enough through your means—but a stop shall soon be put to it The best of aunts shall know—"

"This is very extraordinary indeed!—I came with a full intention of laying before you the inhuman as well as uncivil part you acted by me, and you attack me with furious looks, and menacing gestures. It is true, you have it greatly in your power to injure me with my aunt, and if you can reconcile it to the professions you this afternoon made,—do so Let my aunt know my misfortunes—see me, to whom a few hours ago you seemed a friend, see me, I say, reduced to the abject state, from whence you were by the bounty of my uncle raised. and what praise will the world adjudge you? Reflect, whether it will not be more partial to my indiscreet weakness, than to your premeditated baseness"

"To raise myself upon the ruin of any one, is contrary to my principles perish all those who do! But yet, when I reflect on the past transactions of this day—you must pardon me, Miss Grafton, if I think very hardly of you indeed"

"What indignities you may have borne, I know not, being intirely innocent of them, as Heaven is my judge, and as I can answer it at the last day, I affirm, I know not what you mean When I found myself pretty well recovered, I came into the house, and, upon desiring to be shewn to you, was informed, you had just left it in company with both gentlemen I waited, in hopes you would come back, but not finding you return, and, I must own, a good deal surprized at the oddness of your conduct,

"so

"so different from what I had ever found it, I "ordered a coach to be called, and came directly "hither unable to account for a treatment I little "expected, either from you, or Captain Camp "bell,—as to the other, I even did not ask his "name—I sought an explanation from you."

"Your account is surprisingly strange, and al "most past belief Could you suppose I should "put myself under the protection—or rather in "deed deprive myself of the protection a woman "of virtue claims—and quit the house with two "strange men, leaving you alone there? Though "it would have been better to have gone with the "worst of people, than to remain in it, as it is "a most infamous house

"Infamous! Good God! what could the men "mean by carrying us thither? How have I been "deceived in captain Campbell! but if ever I see "him, I shall convince him I can resent the affront "he has dared to put on women of character."

"Nay, most likely he will be called to account "by the gentleman, as he swore he would oblige "him to clear up an affair which appeared to him "very mystical."

"Did he indeed? Well, but tell me, Caroline, "what happened to you to oblige you to leave the "house, without apprising me of your design, "more especially since you found it to be a bad "one?"

"I was told, you and Campbell were together, "and did not chuse to be interrupted."

"Heavens, what villainy! But sure the wretch "did not dare to take any liberties with you?"

"I tell you, they took us for women of the "town, it is therefore most probable he would "take improper ones, while under the influence of "such an opinion, but he proved himself a man "of honor, when he was undeceived."

"Well,

"Well, I protest, you had like to have been "the heroine of a most delectable adventure Did "not Lord B come into your head? Your spark "did not look as if he could have made use of the "same plea, to evade the sentence of the law"

"You are very jocose upon an affair, which, "had I not met with a man capable of attending "to the dictates of humanity and virtue, I had "by this time been incapable of relating"

I could not help dropping some tears

"Why, you seem as much concerned as if the "greatest of all injuries had been suffered by you"

"Yes! Some people are more alarmed at the "bare apprehension of so great a misfortune, than "many are at the evil itself"

She looked confusedly-conscious, but recovering herself, said, "Do not be low-spirited however, "my dear! The thing cannot transpire, for you "may be certain, Campbell will never mention it, "and the other does not know either of us"

"I am not certain that it will not transpire. for "as I was coming out of the hated house, Sir "George Darnley drove by in his chariot Ah! "my God, should he have seen me, I am un-"done!"—My tears now flowed afresh

"Lord bless me! how can you be so indefati-"gable in tormenting yourself? His view must be "merely transient, and the improbability of seeing "you in such a place, will take off all suspicion, "should he really have recognized you, you may "be certain he will never mention it"

"He shall not need, I will tell him the whole "affair myself"

"If you pause one moment, you must see the "impropriety of such a procedure Will he not "think it very odd to be made your confidant in "such an adventure? You make Sir George of "great consequence, I think. Most men would be "vain of the distinction If you will take my "advice, you will lay aside these things as by no "means eligible It will be time enough, should "he ever mention it, for you then to tell him, by "way of clearing yourself from reproach I can "at the same time vouch for the innocence of your "intentions I shall be happy to have any oppor"tunity of returning any obligations to you the "sense I have of what I owe you, will ever be "very great, however you may think of me"

I consented to her intreaties, and promised not to be the first to mention any thing relative to it.

Mrs G—lton presently came in, we joined her, and spent a very agreeable evening When we parted, I sat down to acquaint you with this strange affair It is too late to make any comment upon it, nor should I know what inferences to draw, had I time Adieu, my dearest Sidney, believe me

Ever your's,

CAROLINE MELMOTH

LETTER LV.

To the Right Honourable the Earl of L

Grosvenor Square, September 4

WHAT a delicious plotter art thou! Fly, my Lord, or the biters will be bitten! keep Campbell out of the way, or he will be forced to betray his trust He is either a knave or fool, I know not whether, but the most glorious scheme that ever was machinated, is thro' his means—blast him for it!—overthrown.

The

The fellow he brought with him, proved a puppy of honor—The honor of the men! Truly he had need have a great ſhare, ſince you rob every woman of it that ye can.

By the addition of mine then, my Lord, I adjure you to keep a watchful eye over this Campbell A ſtupid blockhead! why did he not bring Errington? he had been a man much fitter for our purpoſe Tho' I do not know, if your lordſhip would be ſo well ſatisfied, as I hear he is a very enterpriſing genius, and perhaps would not have permitted your lordſhip—ſo fine an opportunity in his own power—to have *l'entamure* of the devoted fair one Deuce take me for a fool, and all ſuch fools as myſelf, who cannot refuſe a man in the critical moment, but opportunity is the devil Now have you thrown off my ſhackles, and I muſt turn procureſs for your pleaſure, and aſſiſt in rendering this boaſted excellence no better than myſelf For that curſed ſuperiority ſhe aſſumes, or at leaſt ſhe has cauſe to aſſume, from the conſciouſneſs of her own virtue, and the knowledge of my frailty, has determined me to have no reſt, now I have embarked in your cauſe, 'till I have effected mine, and your deſires

Beſides, ſhe has ſtill too much power with my aunt, tho' the means I have taken have in a little degree weakened her influence I trumpt up a ſtory about a legacy my aunt propoſed leaving her, tho' by the bye I find ſhe will have the largeſt ſhare of Madam Grafton's fortune—but intereſt ſeems to have no weight with her

Another thing joined to her knowing me too well, is, ſhe once, ſome years ſince, diſcovered a little plot of mine, which, had it taken effect, would have greatly prejudiced her with her patroneſs, as ſhe fooliſhly ſtyles my aunt She never once took notice of this, after remonſtrating the injury I might have

have done her, in the most gentle terms Now, perhaps you will think it odd, but I have cherished an aversion to her ever since, nor will I rest 'till my revenge is compleat Remember, the Poet says,

Forgiveness to the injured does belong,
But they ne'er pardon, who have done the wrong

Poets are said to paint nature, so I suppose this sentiment to be natural at least, I know it is so with me, and I will pursue it.

I think your lordship is a man of too much spirit to need a stimulus, or I would tell you, my conjectures are true, concerning what I sometime ago hinted to you, of Sir George Darnley's being your rival Yes, it is as true as she is mine I own to you, notwithstanding what has passed between your lordship and me, that Sir George Darnley is the only man that ever truly touched my heart I own I love the dear bewitching Darnley, and 'till this destroyer of my future hopes came in the way, stood fair for engaging his attention O that I may soon see this hated beauty degraded—I beg your pardon for the last expression——but exalted then, if you please, to the enviable title of your lordship's Sultana! And then, then perhaps, when the keen edge of disappointment has worn off, Sir George may again behold me with eyes of tenderness Ah! glorious thought! Think, my dear friend in iniquity, what a charming triumph for both! how shall we at once feast upon love and revenge! Love and revenge, be ye my themes

But you will like to know how my suspicions were confirmed Yesterday, after you left us, I saw Frederick, Darnley's man, give something to Caroline's Abigail ——These Abigails are the very essence of a clandestine amour

I called her into the parlour, and locking the door, charged her, if she would not be turned out of doors inſtantly, to give up what ſhe had juſt received. She at firſt peremptorily denied having any thing, but my threats, and a couple of guineas, at laſt prevailed on her. She begged of me not to break the ſeal, for fear of a diſcovery, but informed me, ſhe generally gave Miſs Melmoth a letter from the ſame quarter every day. I aſked her, what ſhe thought would be her reward, ſhould the lovers ever be united? She anſwered, not much; ſhe feared they would not be ſo generous as they ought, conſidering her fidelity, for that her Lady condemned herſelf for yielding to the ſolicitations of Sir George. I told her to reflect, her reward was precarious, but if ſhe would do as I would adviſe her, her intereſt would be gratified. In ſhort, ſhe had no other alternative, than to be my friend, or be turned out with diſgrace. The wench knew which part to chuſe, and very faithfully diſcloſed to me all ſhe knew of her lady's ſecrets. She ſaid too, ſhe was piqued, for Miſs Melmoth was not like other young ladies in the ſame circumſtance, having never made her acquainted with more, than the frequent intercourſe of letters rendered neceſſary.— Thus have I gained a friend in the enemy's camp, and tho' an under-player, ſhe may be of infinite ſervice. Leave it to me to make ſomething of her.

But, I recollect I told you our ſcheme proved abortive, I will now tell you the particulars: that is, as far as I can.

Caroline is wavering between doubt and uncertainty! She ſtill, notwithſtanding all my perjuries—and I was not ſparing—rather ſuſpects me, tho' ſhe knows not of what. We muſt therefore be more than commonly cautious.

I am now glad you did not make your appearance in the *convenient* houſe: it would moſt probably have put her ſo much upon her guard, as to fruſtrate all our deſigns. Yet as I have laid the plan, should Sir George make inquiries of the people of Bloomsbury, they would but confirm the jealousy which I intend to plant in his breast.

I enforced my arguments with all the money I had in my pocket, and made the old woman swear most devoutly, she would give the proper answers to all questions propos'd about the young lady. I gave her a very accurate description of her person,—for nobody saw her in the house, her fellow commanding them to hide themselves,—and I could perceive my account, tho' not in the most glowing colors, made the old creature grin "a ghastly smile." I make no doubt, she will do every thing in her power to conciliate your Lordship's favour, that she may have the reaping of the second crop, when you are tired of your fair-one, which, with her prudent management, will afford her a plentiful harvest.

Let me see you if possible to morrow.——Remember your behaviour must be very circumspect, guard your expressions, she is tremblingly alive all o'er. Observe to be very assiduous to her, and be as much as possible at her side. Behave to her with a restrained familiarity, especially before Sir George. I should hang myself, were our combinations not to take the desired effect, now they are so ripe.

Upon my soul, I believe you men are the greatest cowards in nature. So soon to be repulsed at last by Miss Melmoth's account of her spark. A pretty fellow too—and one who, Campbell said, was passionately fond of women.

—When all his passions were up in arms—A lovely girl thrown in his—The house—the circumstances all considered—no, I have only her word you know—To be sure, she would keep her own counsel—Who would betray themselves? It would be a cursed thing, if after thus long beating the bush,

bush, you should lose the game You would be ready to cut your throat, should he have taken liberties you would not allow to any but yourself As you are a man of spirit, pursue your advantage She shall be yours tho' all the devils in hell counterplot me. Adieu

Your's faithfully,

L GRAFTON

Some letters from Miss Melmoth to her friend are omitted; not being necessary to the history, and as part of them may be gathered from Miss Vere's letter

---

LETTER LVI

To Miss MELMOTH.

Vere-Park, Sept 13

I Mean to write an answer to the many letters of my beloved Caroline now before me

Your adventure, as you justly style it, needs no other comment, than that Miss Grafton is at the bottom of it Lord L one of her associates Beware of them

But, my dear Caroline, I doubt you are not happy Your last letter particularly gave me great uneasiness There was an affected gaiety which came not from the heart. Two or three lively expressions, and then you sink in the mournful strain You say, " Would to Heaven you were here! I think I stand more in need of a friend than yourself. I am low-spirited —come and raise them

—and yet, I cannot aſk you at this juncture. O Sidney! how unſtable is every ſublunary hope! Nay, we ſcarce know what to wiſh for, ſince the fruition of our wiſhes too often is productive of diſcontent. I could moralize a great while on theſe themes. I have little elſe to do."

You are no cynic, Caroline, to quarrel with the world for nothing: no, you are unhappy, and you refuſe me a participation in your griefs. If you think me worthy of your confidence, unboſom your whole ſoul to me; it will be a relief to you, if no more. Something there is that hangs heavy at your heart. You have not in your laſt letter mentioned Sir George; has he proved unworthy your affections? Tell me, I beſeech you; by our long united loves, tell your Sidney all the truth. I may perhaps have it in my power to alleviate your pain.

I have diſcovered tears on your letter, when you have not recited any thing affecting. My God, you weep and lament—You are low ſpirited—And I not know the cauſe!

Indeed, my love, you muſt repoſe your griefs in the faithful boſom of your Sidney.

My heart is ſo full I can hardly give you an account of a conteſt which I lately held with my father and his ſpouſe. You muſt know, he choſe to publiſh his folly, by taking my lady to the aſſembly at N——. Fine cloaths were made for the occaſion. A few days before the time for ſhewing off, I found the good folks mighty buſy in looking in an eſcrutore. When my father was out of the room, I aſked her, "what ſhe was ſearching there for?"

"For ſomething your father wants, Miſs Vere."

"I take it there is nothing there but what belongs to me. I wonder how the drawers came open: but for the future I ſhall keep them lock-ed."

ed." So ſaying, I took the key out of my pocket, and locked each of the drawers.

My father came in ſoon after. "Sidney," ſaid he, "do you know where your mother kept her jewels?"

"In a private drawer in this eſcrutoire, ſir."

"Which is it?"

I coolly took the key out of my pocket and unlocked it, pulling out an empty drawer. "Here, ſir, is the place where my mother kept them."

"But where are they?"

"In my own cabinet, ſir."

"Let me ſee them."

"If, as I ſuſpect, ſir, you want them to deck out your preſent lady, you muſt excuſe me. They are not family jewels. They were a preſent to my late dear mother before ſhe became your wife. She gave them into my hands ſome time before her death, where they ſhall ever remain."

"How now, confidence! Do you know, ſhe had no right to diſpoſe of any thing without my conſent!"

"Pardon me, ſir, I do know ſhe had an undoubted right; which right ſhe has transferred to me; a right I will never give up to any one. Let the lady you have pleaſed to give the title of my mother-in-law conſider, Virtue is the beſt ornament —Vice would ſully the brighteſt jewels. If ſhe chuſes to dreſs herſelf at my expence, let the ſixty pounds a year which have been deducted from my ſtipend go towards it. But for my bequeathed jewels, I will preſerve them while I have life and underſtanding."

"You are a very bold girl, Sidney. But is it not the ſame thing, if I make you an equivalent?"

"Yes, Sidney, won't that be the ſame thing?"

"My father abridges me in maintenance; you fall in love with my jewels; and I am told that to have, or not to have, is the same thing—Down, down, resentment! I will be patient with the little that is allowed me."

"It is in my power, girl, to make that little less."

"I know it is, sir.—Do what you will, you shall never hear me complain on the subject of money-matters. I shall be of age one time or other, and then I shall have what no one can take from me."

My step-dame said, "I might yet be humbled." I did not think her worth an answer,—but left the room. They have both been upon the sullens ever since. I don't care. My father has taken a wrong method with me. A generous heart may be subdued by generosity—not by meanness. Sixty pounds have been struck of my pension, so I am reduced to half-pay. I must have thirty thousand pounds when I come of age, so the less I spend now, the more I shall have by-and-by; and that will be all they will get by it.

But still, my Caroline, you are uppermost in my thoughts.—Pray write to me soon, and remember there never was a truer friend than your

SIDNEY VERE.

LETTER LVII.

To Miss VERE.

Grosvenor-Square, Sept. 15.

I Must be more circumspect, I see, for the future. I make my Sidney unhappy by surmises. Be under no apprehensions, my best friend. It is true, I have met with some uneasiness—but perhaps it

was

was necessary I might, being too happy, have forgot the source from whence my felicity sprung. But let me give ease to that heart, so dear to your Caroline. I am very happy now,—indeed I am.

I thought I perceived an alteration in Miss Crafton. She no longer, as she was wont, suffered her eyes to dwell on me with maternal affection. Frequently has she been displeased with me for things no one would consider as possible to give offence. A visible coolness—a reserve—took place of that enviable freedom, with which she always treated her hitherto dear Caroline.

To what this change can be owing I do not know, but I hope it will not last. I own it has made me very uneasy.

I have been likewise not quite happy on Sir George Darnley's account. But I am convinced there was no reason in my fears—so no more of it.

I told him the other day, that I was not satisfied with our proceedings. When we conceal our intentions, the world will ever suppose we have reasons for so doing. I hated disingenuity.—We had laid ourselves at the mercy of a servant, who by betraying us, might ruin us for ever.—I said a vast deal to him on this subject.—He was affected with what I advanced. He assured me he would acquaint his mother with his partiality for me. She always expressed so high a regard for me, that he had the less reason to doubt her acquiescence to an affair of so much moment to him. For, continued he, when I convince her, I cannot live without my lovely Caroline, her affection and consideration for an only son, will certainly have weight.

I made no scruple to tell him, I wished him not to delay an affair which became of consequence to my peace of mind. I could not bear to wear the appearance of deceit. I hated to be obliged to conceal my feelings for him.

"Well then," said he, "when next my angel [illegible]s me, I shall fly on the wings of love to her, with [illegible] licence, I hope, in my pocket."

"You are very precipitate indeed," said I, [illegible]. "But do not you think I shall put in a [illegible] to postpone affairs a little?"

"No," replied he, gazing on me with transport [illegible], and pressing my hand with tenderness [illegible]. "No, I am too well acquainted with the [illegible] Caroline, to suspect she [illegible] a heart devot'd to her."

We had no opportunity for any further conversation.

[illegible] It is true, I have [illegible] to be displeased with his behaviour [illegible] the least degree respectful. But he is so very [illegible]—so ready to do me every little service—I could readily excuse him. If he is sincere in his love professions to me, I very much pity him—yet I wish he would not come here so [illegible].

Where-ever we go, we always meet him; and, [illegible] he singles me out to hear his re[illegible].

I am always sorry, my dear, when you have any contention with your father. And yet I hardly know how to blame you. I am certain you would [illegible] have given up double the value of the jewels with pleasure. But these were the gift of an amiable and beloved mother. Were they common baubles, they would for that reason have been highly estimated by you.

I [illegible] all I think on your observations. Had your father been as amiable as your mother, you would have been an exemplary daughter.—But remember, my best love, a little consideration in you for him, may excite more tender returns.

CAROLINE MELMOTH

To

To Miss VERE, in Continuation.

Sept. 16. Twelve, midnight.

I think every thing I have undertaken, has lately fallen out adverse; I believe it is a punishment for my correspondence with Sir George Darnley. You know how I have ever condemned the least appearance of dissimulation, but had not resolution or power however to prevent its still continuing. It has involved me in disagreeable circumstances. Certain it is, the commission of one error leads to many others,—which are, in consequence of the first, unavoidable. I have been constrained to tell an untruth, and now to prevent the detection of the first falsehood, I must sacrifice my veracity again. How hateful—how perplexing to a mind not disingenuous, is such a situation! Heaven grant I may safely extricate myself out of this affair, and if ever I write, or again receive a letter from him in a clandestine manner, may the worst of evils light on me!

Sir George, in a billet this morning, told me, he wished I would contrive to meet him either in the Park or the Grove this afternoon. Walking might easily be proposed—and our meeting there nothing remarkable. At dinner, Mrs. Grafton observed it was very pleasant, and she should like an airing. I asked her if a walk would be disagreeable to her, instead of a ride? She said, if we intended to walk in the Park, she would be of our party for a little time.

Mrs. Grafton's going with us, I knew would make no difference to Sir George, as he had less reason to be on the reserve, since he had resolved to acquaint Lady Darnley, and consequently Mrs. Grafton, with his attachment to me.

We separated as we usually do after dinner. I went to my closet, and took a book to read. Jenny came up to me, and shutting the door, began:

"I stepped out just as dinner was served, madam, to enquire of the clear-starcher, if she had finished your linen; and as I was crossing South Audley-Street, who should I see but Sir George Darnley.—He stopped me. I think myself very fortunate to meet you, said he, I was just going into the next coffee-house, to write a note to your lady. I am prevented being in the Park this evening, where she promised to meet me: but I must see her.—Tell her, if she will be so kind as to give me the meeting any where but at Mrs Grafton's, the opportunity will make me very happy."——

"Good God!" interrupted I, "What could Sir George—"

"So I told him, madam. Lord sir," said I, "does your honor think my young lady will consent to meet you in a strange place?" "My dear Jenny," answer'd Sir George, "you mistake me.—Can you imagine I would solicit my beloved angel to any action which is improper? No: I love her too well. But tell your charming mistress, something of consequence has happened, which I wish to consult her upon.—I could indeed write to her, but that would not be sufficient, as I much want to have her opinion on the affair in question.—I have a thousand things to say to her.—I shall have no opportunity to see her 'till after to-morrow." "Well then, Sir George," said I, "if my lady consents to meet your honor, where is it to be?" "I will tell you Jenny. I am engaged to dine at the Thatched-house; but I will make an excuse to get away for an hour or two: if Miss Melmoth will be so kind as to come, as it by accident, to the Italian Warehouse in the Hay-Market,—or to Pinchbeck's Repository, or to Bellis's in Pall-Mall."

"Love

"Love will provide her with a pretence to avoid accompanying Miſs Grafton in a walk,—ſhould they have fixed on going. Caution her, my good Jenny, to act with great circumſpection, as I have reaſon to believe Miſs Grafton is not much her friend."

"I took the liberty, madam, to anſwer for you, that you would be at Bellis's at ſeven in the evening. I thought you would better approve that place, than either of the others."

"I do not know what to think of this buſineſs, Jenny, I wiſh you had not poſitively ſaid I would meet Sir George.—It is an intricate affair.—What can he have to ſay to me?—of ſuch conſequence too.—That alone diſtreſſes me, and fills me with a thouſand fears."

"Moſt likely, madam, Sir George may have ſpoken to lady Darnley, and her ladyſhip refuſed her conſent.—or perhaps he may have made ſome diſcovery about Miſs Grafton.—I know as well as any thing, ſhe is a ſecret enemy.—for ſhe envies you the preference ſhewn you by every-body."

"I have often told you, Jenny, and I expect to be obeyed, never to make any diſreſpectful reflections on Miſs Grafton.—I know your pique to her. I forbid you ever in my preſence to ſay a word againſt her."

"Well, madam, I have done," was her pert anſwer. And away ſhe went muttering, "ſhe knew ſome folks, better than ſome folks thought." I took no notice of it. I never pay any attention to thoſe aſides.

I ſat myſelf down to conſider how I ſhould adjuſt this affair. I had a conflict with myſelf, on what I ſhould determine,—but at laſt love gained the victory over prudence.—I could not offend Miſs Grafton, becauſe no inconvenience could accrue to her, beſides ſhe could not know it.—Pretty ſophiſ-

try

tr this! but such as it was, it surmounted every difficulty, when put in competition with disappointing Sir George.—Curiosity too came in for its share.

Mrs. Grafton proposed drinking tea with a lady in Stanhope-Street, and going from thence to the Park. I begged she would excuse my attending her, as I had a head-ache, which had encreased considerably since dinner."

"I am sorry your head aches," said Miss Grafton, "but are you sure you have no other reason?"

I believe I looked confused a little, but I attributed it to her unkind suspicion.—And said, "Had she been indisposed, I should have afforded her my pity at least."

"I can do more," answered she, "I can afford you my company."

"Yes," said Mrs. Grafton, "since you are not able to go, my dear, we can put off the visit to another time. Letty, will you be so kind as to forbid the coach? My dear Caroline, smell at my eau-de-luce."

"My dear madam," said I, "do not let my disorder prevent your evening's walk. I shall be quite unhappy, if you should on my account lose the benefit of so fine an evening.—Miss Grafton too will never forgive me. Let me intreat you, madam." I at last prevailed on them to go.

When they had driven from the door, Jenny came into the parlour with my hat and cloak.

"You are in a great hurry, Jenny."

"Consider, madam, it is a great way to Pall-Mall, and I see it is six o'clock, and past."

"Well," said I, in a dissatisfied tone, "how are we to go?"

"Why, madam, if you will slip out presently after me, I will secure the first hack I can find."

I agreed to her proposal.—She went.—I soon followed, and at the bottom of the first street, saw a coach a coach driving slowly. Jenny beckoned to the man, and we both stepped in; I had determined to take her with me.

She bade the man drive to Pall-Mall, as fast as possible. He obeyed her commands, with so much alacrity, that by the time we reached the end of Old-Bond-street, the main brace of the coach broke, and we were thrown over. I was a little hurt, but infinitely more frightened! I shrieked involuntarily, and Jenny screamed with great violence.

With some difficulty we were disengaged from the shattered machine. The people gathered round us immediately, some offering their assistance—some advising me to take the number of the coach, that the fellow might be punished—others asking where I came from, and where I was going. In the midst of this confusion, Lord L's chariot drove along Piccadilly. His coachman seeing the croud checked the horses, and Lord L presently distinguished me, who by this time had got upon the foot-way leaning on Jenny's arm.

He instantly leaped from the chariot, without staying for the servant to open the door, and hastening up to me, "expressed his concern and surprise at seeing me in such a situation,—and begged I would command his chariot to convey me home."

"I thanked him for his obliging offer, but declined it, saying, I was going further."

"Further! Good Heavens! you look ready to faint now.—Let me prevail on you to go into this milliner's, and take a few drops.—What blood is this?—My God, you have cut your arm!"

"It is a trifle.—Nothing at all—I do not mind it."

"You must have some remedy." He took out his handkerchief and bound round it. I would readily have compounded for a much worse accident

any

an other time I felt myself very sensibly chagrin-ed I knew not how to act with regard to Lo L Had I owned I had been on a secret expedition it would have given room for injurious suspicion of me in a man who wants no encouragement to be troublesome, besides, laying me under an obligation or I did not chuse to owe him above all men this on one hand presented it self to me,—on the other side, was the apprehension of his betraying me to Mrs Grafton, by the inquiries he would undoubtedly make, unless prevented —I told him, "I was tolerably recovered by the help of my eau-de-luce and was obliged to him for his care Telling him likewise, I would take a chair to convey me whither I was going"

He expressed his astonishment at my having been in a hackney-coach, unattended but by my maid

I endeavoured to stop his inquisitiveness,—so told him a frivolous tale, and likewise begged him not to take notice of the accident which happened, as Mrs Grafton would be uneasy on my account

He promised he would be very cautious, if I would suffer him to attend me home

I again informed him, I had other business. He continued to insist on the impropriety of attempting to go any where but home ——"Look at your dress —what would the people where you are going think, if you conceal the occasion of this blood and dirt upon your gown? and your confessing the cause will render you liable to Mrs Grafton's discovery of the accident"

"Those to whom I am going, will excuse the disorder"

"I have done, madam —Indeed I might, had I not been the greatest dunce, surmised to whom a young lady of condition, attended only by her maid, in a hackney-coach, was going —But I beg your pardon, madam, for detaining you so long"

"For

"For Heavens-ſake, madam," cried Jenny, "do not let my lord go away with ſuch a ſuſpicion."

"You do me great injuſtice, my lord, in harbouring ſuch thoughts of me.—I am conſcious of no bad purpoſe.—But as it grows late, will defer my viſit: this accident will be a ſufficient excuſe for my non-performance."

"Then, madam, you will do me the honour of accepting a place in my chariot,—you will ſurely have no inclination to venture yourſelf a ſecond time in a hackney coach."

I continued peremptorily to refuſe him, and to ſtrengthen my refuſal, pleaded my having my maid with me.

That ſhould be no obſtacle, he ſaid, for he would wait at a coffee-houſe 'till the chariot returned, which ſhould then take him to Park-Street, where he was engaged to be at eight o'clock.

I told him, "it would be very abſurd in me, by a ridiculous punctilio, to riſk his lordſhip's being too late."

Jenny ſaid, "Indeed, madam, you had better accept my Lord L—'s offer. I will, with your leave, ſtep to the place where you was to have called, leſt they ſhould be under any apprehenſions on your account."

I at laſt conſented, and my lord conducted me ſafely hither. Our converſation was of no conſequence.—But little on my ſide. I could not help reflecting on the circumſtances of the afternoon: nor did the retroſpect afford me much pleaſure: on the contrary, I was exceedingly mortified.—My ſituation was to the laſt degree perplexing, which was augmented on my return, by my being conſtrained either to change my cloaths, or by the condition they were in, hazard a diſcovery.

Not that there was really any crime in my going out,—but the myſterious manner of it.—Nothing ſhall

shall ever tempt me for the future to deviate in the most trivial circumstance from truth.

I despise myself for being guilty of this action. I seem contemptible in my own eyes, and I dread lest Sir George may not some time hence condemn his wife, for the dissimulation he occasioned in his mistress.

I blamed myself for every transaction that had passed, but as they had passed they could not be recalled, nor could I recede. Thus are we drawn on to tell a thousand falsehoods to conceal one. Jenny persuaded me to feign myself still worse, and go to bed, saying, she would take upon herself to acquaint Mrs Grafton of my increasing indisposition. Accordingly, I went into bed about nine.—The ladies came home soon after. Being apprized by Jenny of my illness, they came up stairs. I complained of the pain in my head. Mrs Grafton seemed much concerned, and prescribed some whey to me, which however I declined, saying, "I hoped a good night's rest would quite recover me." They joined in wishing it me, and retired.

My thoughts were too confused to suffer me to rest. I could hardly support Mrs Grafton's tender inquiries: it was the first time I thought myself wholly unworthy them.—I had deceived her.—My reflections were too keen, I burst into tears; they could not wash away the sense of my dissimulation. I rose, and, partly dressing myself, sought relief by pouring my whole soul out to my Sidney. I am sensible I shall incur your blame, but I am certain your censures will be infinitely lighter than those I bestow on myself.

In consequence of the resolution I have taken, I have not informed Sir George by line or message. I hope he will excuse it: if he loves me truly, I know he must.

Who

Who would ever deviate from the strictest rules, if they suffered for it in their minds as I do! Adieu, my beloved Sidney.

Yours for ever,

CAROLINE MELMOTH.

LETTER LVIII.

To the Earl of L——

Sept. 15.

OUR scheme, I find by Jenny, has succeeded to our wish. I have testimony enough, I think now, to ruin my rival in Sir George's esteem; every thing else for you must fall out of course.

How prettily the gudgeon swallowed the bait of a message from her swain!—While he, nothing suspecting but his Dulcinea would be in the Park, met us there in high spirits,—which were however a little damped, when Mrs Grafton told him of his dearee's indisposition.

I took care to let him know our intention of staying with her, but that she would by no means permit us.

He walked with us some time, and on leaving us, said he would call to-morrow and inquire of Miss Melmoth's health.

I have taken a precaution which I hope will prevent their meeting.—Alone they shall never be.

Matters are now coming about:—my chief business will be to prevent explanations of every sort.

I am almost afraid you are doubtful of success; when last we met, you said, you thought her virtuous on principle.—I laugh at your sentiments.—Believe me, my lord, they are Utopian. What temptation

temptation has ſhe had to renounce her virtue? Beloved, adored by the moſt lovely of men—ſ ... ted to marriage—where has been the trial?— ... my lord, I hope to have you ſoon convince ... my creed, that when a woman's reputation is ... her virtue ſinks from the ſight. Once degr... and ſhe will fall—fall, never to riſe again!

It is now time, my lord, for us to play ... laſt ſtake. I have poiſoned my aunt's mind ... will ſoon work. She ſtill has great partiality fo... favorite, but I truſt, in a few days ſhe will th... it more meritorious to diſcard her for ever from ... preſence, than ever ſhe did in ſuccouring her ... ſhort, we may, I think, ſtrike the laſt ſtr... which muſt effectually throw her on your pro... en,—being deprived of all other. I am imp... to have all finiſhed.

I think it adviſable that you ſhould write a le... as if to Miſs Melmoth, which ſent to me I ... drop in her dreſſing-room, wherein you may me... on your meeting as this day, at the old lady's ... Bloomſbury; it will be corroboration of Jen... evidence, which ſhe is ready to give, of Carol... going out this afternoon for that purpoſe.

Caroline cannot ſee Sir George theſe two day... my management, by that time, I hope every th... will be ſettled to your wiſhes, and thoſe of

Your lordſhip's

faithful adherent,

L. GRAF...

B...

Billet to Lord L.

Sept 16

Sir George has been here every thing is in the right train—The amanuensis you sent, is admirable Darnley is ripe for receiving every impression I cannot tell you how the poison was administered, but it worked purely—I revere your scheme at the tavern,—and almost envy your superior genius—I have not time to write—I am all rapturous expectation. To morrow night—make but that mine, and fate do thy worst.—Adieu.

LETTER LIX.

To Miss Vere

Grosvenor-Square, Sept 17

I HAVE not seen Sir George Darnley, since the risque I ran to meet him "He sent me an apology, and his most tender inquiries by Jenny, he told her, he intended that very day to acquaint his mother with his intentions — Begged I would not stay away from St James's-Square, as his family had remarked I was a great stranger lately"

Mrs Grafton and her niece went out this morning they are not yet returned Were I not willing to hope, I should give way to a thousand apprehensions, as I fear I must tell you, Mrs Grafton within these two days has amazingly cooled in her behaviour to me Miss Grafton, who carries herself towards me with a kind of forced civility,

never

never gives me an opportunity, if I could avail myſelf of one, to requeſt how I have offended —I wiſh I could ſhake off this weight from my ſpirits —I will try to be cheerful

Mrs Grafton ſent me word, Lady Alicia Montague had preſſed her to ſtay dinner —

I think I will go to Lady Darnley's this afternoon It ſeems long ſince I have ſeen my dear Darnley I hope we ſhall ſoon talk over, and laugh at, the difficulties we have gone through —The reflection of paſt griefs heightens preſent joys

I recollect, this evening Lady Darnley gone to company, but no matter, I ſhall only make little alteration in my dreſs

The thoughts of going thither have raiſed my ſpirits I may perhaps write a little more when I return adieu for the preſent —

Eight o'clock

Where are now my happy proſpects! All, vaniſhed!—Yes my Sidney, the golden dream all over —Your Caroline is wretched, wretched beyond hope —How ſhall I tell you—how find words to paint my diſtreſs!

My tears obliterate the traces of my pen —what have I elſe to do than weep!

I went, O my God! went to Lady Darnley full of ſpirits— No *preſentiment* of what would happen

When Henry aſked the porter if Lady Darnley was at home, he anſwered, ſhe was not, with ſome degree of heſitation of which however I took little notice, but Frederic coming up, ſaid, " Yes my lady is at home, what do you mean ?" to the porter, who muttered ſomething, which I paid no attention to I went up ſtairs preceded by Frederic who announced my name " Miſs Melmoth, my la[dy] lady."—"Miſs Melmoth!" I heard a voice exclaim, "ſure not!" By this time I entered the room, and approached to pay my *devoir* to Lady Darnley.

She looked very formal at me, but my attention was taken up, for I obſerved juſt as I came in, Sir George went out at the other door.

A profound ſilence enſued for ſome time; at laſt I ventured to break it by ſpeaking to a lady next me, upon which, ſhe turned herſelf immediately from me, and aſked ſome trifling queſtion of her next neighbour, not deigning even to look at me.

I quitted my ſeat for one next Miſs Harriot Darnley; I ſpoke to her, and received the moſt chilling anſwer. It almoſt overcame me. "For God's ſake, Miſs Harriot, what does this treatment of me mean——and how am I to account for it?" "You can give the beſt interpretation," ſhe returned ſcornfully.—"Some people's inſolence—" in a half-whiſper,---and addreſſing herſelf to Miſs Hamilton, who ſat on the other ſide,—"Well, what was you ſaying of the opera?"

I ſaw I was to be ſhaken off.—Upon which, I ſaid, "I ſee a great alteration in thoſe I once thought honored me with their friendſhip;—but this is no place for any explanation.—Shall I intreat the favor of your ladyſhip"—to Lady Darnley,—"to ring the bell."

She bowed, and rang it,—Frederick came in.

"Be ſo kind, ſir, as to order me a chair."

"Your ſervant, madam, is not here."

"No matter. Pray let me have a chair." I aroſe. "The next time I have the honor to wait on your ladyſhip—perpaps—this"—I could not utter any more. Tears guſhed into my eyes.—I courtſeyed, and left the drawing-room. I ſaw Sir George paſſing the antichamber. His arms were folded. "Tell me, for Heaven-ſake tell me, what

I have

I have done. O, Darnley! how have I deserv'd this?"—Tears would not suffer me to proceed.

"Can you aſk me, perfidious woman?" He was inſtantly gone.

I know not how I got down ſtairs. Frede- was there, a chair ready.—I threw myſelf into it. I endeavoured to conceal my tears:—the ſervant perceived my diſtreſs,—he appeared moved, and ſighed.——The leaſt compaſſion to one before treated with cruelty affects greatly. I could not then reſtrain my tears. The men ſhut the top; ah! would it had cloſed me up for ever!——

O Sidney, I muſt complain.——They conveyed me hither, and here I am with a broken heart. What miſery have I ſtill to encounter! No, ſurely, there cannot more be allotted me;——if there is, I muſt ſink under it.

O Darnley! where are all thy vows of laſting love?---broken, with my peace.

Mrs Grafton is not yet come home.--Ah! how ſhall I be able to ſee her! O my Sidney! loſt yet.

CAROLINE MELMOTH.

LETTER LX.

To WILLIAM STANHOPE, Esq;

St James's-Square, Sept 19.

JOIN with me, Stanhope, in execrating the whole perfidious ſex.—Perdition ſeize them! O Stanhope, the dear, the lovely Caroline, is falſe—vile—infamous!

I muſt

I mentioned some incidents which gave me uneasiness. How has every corroborating circumstance concurred to remove the mist of passion from my eyes, and shew me woman, dissembling, artful woman! Remove the mist of passion did I say? Ah! no. I still love her, to madness love her. Why can I not tear her from my heart, as she is for ever wrested from my esteem. In my faithful bosom they were firmly connected.

How am I deceived! how punished for my almost adoration of this seeming masterpiece of nature!

It is to Miss Grafton—Heaven reward her! to whom I owe the discovery of the vile artful creature!

O Stanhope! what a wound has your friend received! My mother and sisters were not inclined to an union with this unhappy creature, tho' they, like me, were deceived by her semblance of innocence.—O, she might have deceived an angel! What death to all my fond hopes!—Heaven can only know with what purity I loved her!

The first suggestions which occurred to me, were of getting her from her paramour, keeping her 'till I was sated with her beauties, and then abandoning her to all the miseries of a prostitute life. Sudden revenge urged this: but soon reason triumphed, and I despised my rash plan. What pleasure could I reap from the possession of her person alone? That to me, was but her second charm.—I loved her mind.—Beautiful as was her outward form, the virtues which inhabited her soul, and beam'd from her lovely eyes, attracted me infinitely more. By Heaven, my passion disgusted her, it partook too much of sentiment for her gross desires.

—Yet, must I relinquish all my fond, long-indulged wishes?—I must.—What shall I do? I would

fly

fly to you, Stanhope, but my soul still keeps ver me about this town.—I cannot quit it—for C—Caroline, the faithless perjured Caroline, ho its every faculty.—She is in lodgings, taken b C[illegible] keeper.

Poor Mr. Grafton is greatly to be pitied— ill, I hear, owing to the discovery of this sham ful intrigue.—What then is to become of Darnley?—

—I must see Caroline,—just to upbraid her— more, and then farewel to England.—O th could as easily lay down life! for have I no all that can make it desirable? What can the due be, but protracted misery?

In the first moments of my despair, I sought lief from the bottle, and buried my griefs for while; but oh! I found it in vain—they retu ed with double force, and convinced me it was in the power of dissipation to mitigate my pain

My pride too is wounded—that may help support the agonizing torture of a broken he Ah! how miserable has the knowledge of her ba ne's left me! Would I had been always deceived that I might by this time have been the husband of th t?—Pride, I thank thee for that suggestio—And yet my fancy paints her, what she appea in my fond doating eyes.—Ungrateful, licentio woman! Stanhope, I will tear her from my hear—I have done for ever with the sex. No mo will I be caught in their snares.—They are all ce tful—from my soul I abjure them for eve Adieu.

Your's,

GEORGE DARNLEY.

LET

LETTER LXI

To Miss Vere.

Sept. 23.

YOU will not wonder at my silence for a week after my last melancholy letter, which was but as a prologue to the most dreadful tragedy.---- Yes, Sidney, my ruin is now complete.

The evils of this life I cease to wonder at, but that human nature can exist under such calamities, is still my astonishment. Ah! who would have gained my belief, by telling me a few months ago, that Caroline Melmoth could have survived the miseries she has experienced, and live to relate them!——Where is there hope! All is fled, and I, a wretched outcast, am fled to deplore for ever the blissful scenes I once beheld, and be deprived of them eternally!

Will you still, thou best of friends, behold with a favourable eye, the unhappy victim of treachery and fraud?---Branded with infamy, ingratitude, and every crime my soul abhors? Will you still suffer the partiality for your poor Caroline, to exist in the most generous of bosoms? Tho' all the world be against me, will my Sidney still be my friend? Ah! can she? Can virtue hold converse with one, who is abandoned by a cruel world to infamy and want?---Oh! can I bear the reflection! My name tainted,--stiled infamous!---ungrateful! ungrateful to the best of women--false to the sincerest of men!---Turned out of doors!---Can I then hope, if my dearest friend listens to the dictates of prudence, she will countenance such a wretch?---But is my Sidney then, a time-serving friend?

Is she not eminently superior to those, who ... ... that glorious sentiment? I will not then ... ---But O! if you ever loved me, ease my ... and give the only consolation my wretched ... is capable of tasting

I will endeavour to acquaint you with the ... particulars of the ruin which overwhelmed me

After the dreadful reception I met from the L... ... family, I waited with great anxiety for the ... of Mrs Grafton I had wept incessantly ... the time of coming home About ten, when I ... finished my letter to you, I went down into ... parlour; my mind under the most dreadful ... from an unhappy presage of something worse, little did I imagine what that something would ... I continued there near an hour, but no appe... of the ladies, a circumstance altogether singular

Tired of every place, I went up to my ... room, and sitting down at the table, was beginni... —or rather continuing,—a retrospect of the ev... of the day I began mechanically to undress m... self, not with a view of going to bed, for I co... not hope to rest I had taken off my cap, tipp... and stomacher, when I heard a loud rap at ... door Presently Mrs and Miss Grafton came to my room, and demanded in a peremptory m... ner to be let in I was greatly agitated, but w... to the door, and drawing the bolt, opened it ... trembled and turned pale, at seeing the cou... nances of my once kind benefactress, and her ... ral companion,—tho' they were very different ...

Mrs Grafton began in a tone of voice not u... to her "Is it thus, Caroline, you have repaid my tenderness? But why do I seek to expostul... with such an abandoned, infamous wretch?"

"How have I deserved these cruel epithe... said I, ready to sink with terror and grief "I...

in what, dear madam, have I been so wretched to offend you?"

"Ask me not what you can resolve yourself. Do you know this hand, vile creature?"—Throwing me a note wrote to the villain Lord L in which, as if from me, I told him my affair with Sir George was near concluded, the thoughts of which made me happy, as it was sufficient it should be so for my reputation. It contained some sarcasms both on Miss and Mrs Grafton, and concluded with an appointment as usual for that night.—The hand appeared exactly mine.

I remained with my eyes riveted to the paper, without motion, till roused by Miss Grafton's saying, "Conscious guilt, you see, madam, needs no accuser. Now, my pretty miss Sanctity, will you swear your infamous paramour has not kept his appointment? I have a strange *presentiment* the accomplice in this pretty intrigue is not far off."---And was moving towards the bed.

"First tell me," said I firmly, "by what right you dare to presume to make this search? But I fear you not---I may meet with protection where you little think. But to you, madam," turning to Mrs Grafton, weeping, "I have long with deep concern seen an alteration in your behaviour to me, tho' certainly your kindness infinitely surpassed my deserts. But why, if you chose to part with me, why would you so change your noble nature, as to seek to ruin me! Ah, is it not sufficient for the unhappy wretch at your feet"---(I knelt to her---"that she loses the happiness of your esteem, but she must be made to feel the dreadfullest of all ills, the loss of reputation? And can you,---you who have suffered your eyes to dwell on me with delight,---can you consent to see me lost, abandoned to the wide world? Where have I a friend if you throw me off? Send me far from you, if I am grown h tell to you ---I never wished or expected gre a ours; but do not, ah! do not deprive me your esteem ----Do not join with the worst wretches, to break a heart already pierced with deepest woe."---My sobs choaked my voice.

"That I once loved you" said the dear, b of women, "that my soul doated on you, Ca ne, let my every action testify, nay to the wron g of that good girl there."

"Would to Heaven you had never deceived me or that the deception (so weak am I,) had con ued all my life. I do not condemn you from pearances only, it is from the conviction of cr crimes, crimes which make me shudder not on to give yourself up to a vicious course, but to e deavour to draw in the heir of a noble family, to a cloak to conceal it, are crimes, were I to forgive I should become a participater of. You are you you may see and repent these enormities. But is the last time I will ever behold you. Ah, co I once imagine, I could receive satisfaction in su a resolution!"

"Now, madam," said Miss Grafton, with sneer, "you may see, the farce is over." came up to me as if to assist me. "Stand monster!" I exclaimed, "nor come near me."

"You said, my dear madam, you had not co demned me without proof---But where are my cusers? Bring them to me."

"This is one," said Miss Grafton, who seem to take pleasure in mortifying me more sensibl and produced my maid. "I caught this girl re ceiving a letter from Lord L.'s footman. I threat ed her, if she did not give it up to me; after long contest, she did. I represented to her the h nous crime she was guilty of, in conniving a shocking and infamous an intrigue. She this gave me the letter my aunt shewed you, and wh you cannot with all your arts deny to be your own hand-writing."

"Eternal providence! Is it possible you can vent such horrid falsehoods? Great Heaven! what will become of me! Whither shall I go, to assert my innocence?"

"By Heavens!" exclaimed Lord L bursting from my closet, "I will not, cannot longer support my lovely angel [illegible] treated in this manner.--- Here, my [illegible] Caroline, shall you find protection---I will give it you."---"Unhand me, villain!" cried I, gasping out of breath. "Gracious powers, protect me!" I fell insensible on the floor ---Too soon I recovered to sense and misery. O my Sidney, here was a plot!---The vile Lord L with the utmost grimace, reviled his infernal agent, and irritated Mrs Grafton more against me. "It is thus," said she, rage sparkling in her eyes, "it is thus you assert your innocence?"---I could not speak.---"Regard it not," said the horrid monster, "in these arms you shall ever find an asylum: come with me---suffer me to take you from a house where you have been so ill-used."

When I recovered my speech I again besought my once kind benefactress to believe me innocent: and yet how strong were appearances against me!

Miss Grafton begged her aunt to turn us both out of the house together, as only fit company for each other.

"Rise!" said Mrs Grafton, "and follow your vile associate, under this roof you shall no longer remain."

"In pity kill me, madam, but do not drive me from your presence with this hated wretch: no power on earth shall oblige me to go with him. My soul, ever since I knew his vices, has abhorred him ---You said, I was young, and might repent: ah! do not then, Madam, admitting I am guilty, precipitate me ſtill lower in the depths of ſin---B you will one day, when perhaps my ſorrows ha killed me---know me innocent of theſe hei crimes, and then you will lament, tho' too la this harſh treatment.

"I aſk no other favour, than to remain this o night under this hoſpitable roof, early to-morro the moſt wretched of her ſex will leave you, ne again to appear in your much-loved preſence. Yo memory, harſhly as I am uſed, will be ever dear me."

Mrs. Grafton appeared moved, and graciou condeſcended to grant my requeſt.---The inſtant Lord L--- took leave of us, "begging me not impute to him the curſed miſchance, which h only for a time retarded our joys."

When he was gone, Mrs. Grafton ſaid, "I lo upon it as a proof you are not quite abandoned vice, in that you refuſed to accompany Lord L--."

"But how will you know ſhe does not go him to-morrow, aunt?"

Mrs. Grafton paid very little attention to h niece's queſtion, but addreſſing herſelf to me, pr ceeded. "I ſhould hope, in return for ſome li favours I have ſhewn you, you will not wound m heart, by ſeeing the child whom I fondly loved," and the tears rolled down her venerable cheeks- "kill me not with beholding you herd among th common wretches, whoſe life you have choſen.-- I could not ſupport ſuch a ſight.---I will give you chance of not being, tho' neceſſitous circumſtanc conſtrained to ſeek ſubſiſtence in infamy. Eve thing you hitherto called your own, ſhall be your together with a limited ſum, for which you m draw on my banker."

[Here, my dear Sidney, was unexampled goo neſs in my dear patroneſs, conſidering the light i which ſhe viewed me.]

I agr

I again threw myself at her feet, overwhelmed with the sense of her goodness—I wept aloud—At last, in broken accents, and frequent sobs, "If, my dearest Madam, you can believe me the wretch I am represented, consign me to the perdition I deserve. Leave me naked—friendless—as the bounty of the best of men found me.—Dreadful as is my distress, it is yet augmented on the reflection of what pangs will rend your breast, on the knowledge of the injuries I have received.—But Oh! Madam, your unprecedented goodness overcomes me. Vile as I appear in your eyes, it is the attribute of angels. But I cannot, dare not avail myself of your innate generosity—I leave you, Madam," rising,—"with a heart overflowing with gratitude—Never shall I cease to pray for your welfare, or ever cease to remember your unbounded love, while you thought me worthy. God forgive those who have suggested other thoughts!"

She left the room in great emotion. How my heart was pierced! I thought, when I no longer beheld her, my life was fled. I threw myself in a chair, and leaning my head on my hands, poured forth a torrent of tears.

The ill-natured wretch, who had caused my misery, insulted me to the highest degree, but my soul was too full to lose a thought upon so despicable a creature: and yet, vile as she is, she triumphs in my wretchedness. She at length left me, to lament my sorrows alone.

I spent the night in fruitlessly moaning my hard destiny, and collecting my cloaths. I did not think there was any occasion to leave them behind me, as nobody would wear them, and as it would be thought I could get others elsewhere.

The vile Jenny offered to assist me, but I ordered her from my sight, unless she was to see I took nothing but what belonged to me. Perhaps I spoke with too much acrimony, considering her as on an implement in the hands of the most w wretches — but I hardly knew what I said

In the morning I rang the bell, and sent a note t Mrs Grafton, full of the most grateful acknowledg ments my heart in every line of it "I begg permission to throw myself once more at her fe and protest my innocence, adding, if I had n been too tender to the faults of others, I should n now have suffered by their malice"

Mrs Grafton in a few minutes came into th room, and in an ironical way complimented upon my address, and concluded with saying, "it great was very eloquent, tho' it failed at present"

"Sir," said I, with the greatest air of contemp I could assume, "if Mrs Grafton would not d an answer to my humble request, she might have spared me the pain of beholding her, who been the cause of all my afflictions You may t triumph over the unhappy victim of your treacher and trample on all laws, human and divine — time I have here to stay, is very short, render yet more disagreeable by your hated presence"

She pretended she would yet be my friend

"I detest both you and your offers of friend ship —You cannot injure me more than you have done —Again I cannot be deceived in you —You know once it was in my power, lately, by speaking the truth, to have ruined you with your aunt—but my heart disdained it—as it does thee—and all that is base"

I desired to have a coach called —My boxes were put into it, and I went down stairs, my heart ready to break

The parlour-door was hastily shut and locked, to prevent any attempt to see Mrs Grafton

I threw myself into the coach, and ordered to be carried to Gerrard-street, where Mrs Johnson lodges

lodges When I arrived there, I found she had set off the day before for St Albans, her sister, who lives there, being dangerously ill, had sent express for her The woman of the house likewise informed me, Mrs Johnson had given up her lodging for some time to her, and that they were let to a family every day expected in town

This was a new misfortune to me I knew not what course to take I wept as if I had been unused to disappointment —I begged to remain there some time, 'till I could send a messenger to St. Albans —The woman said she was sorry she could not oblige me, but that every room in the house was taken, except that which she herself occupied —Immediately the housekeeper, or some such person, came down into the parlour, and said, as the family were not to come for a few days, I should be extremely welcome to stay till the return of the messenger, or that her master came up I thought it the better way to accept of her offer She conducted me up stairs into a bed-chamber I begged she would leave me —I flung myself on the bed, and indulged the utmost grief —I would have wrote to you, but I found my head so confused, that several times I knew not where I was —At last I fell into a doze, or at least a state of insensibility— and when I awoke, I found myself very feverish, which increased, and in a few hours I was in a high fever and delirious They took great care of me during my illness, which obliged me to keep abed several days I have not yet left my chamber —

—Ah! Sidney, why did I recover! Why did not death prevent the ills I may yet suffer! Yet what can happen worse than I have already experienced No It is not in nature to pour forth more Spiels, surely I have had my portion

I thought it most advisable to change my name Alas! what pretensions have I to the name of Melmoth?

moth? But I would forget every thing that has passed as the most likely method to regain a state of peace

I have not yet been able to settle any plan for my future proceedings—I have dispatched a man and horse to Mrs Johnson, I hope her sister will be able to dispence with her attendance

I wonder the people who have taken the lodgings, are not yet come

When you favour me with a letter, direct it by the name of Middleton, at Mrs Wilson's, Gerrard-street, Soho

Adieu, my dearest Sidney, continue to love

Your unfortunate

CAROLINE MELMOTH

LETTER LXII

To Miss MELMOTH, superscribed to Mrs MIDDLETON

Vere-Park, Sep 25

HOW great are your sufferings, my dear, my ever amiable Caroline! Think not your Sidney's heart can hear unmoved your afflictions—no, they sink deep I weep incessantly for your distress—Ten thousand times more I feel it too because not in my power to alleviate it To a you, I feel, I weep your unparalleled misfortunes is all left your poor Sidney. I cannot offer you an asylum

Fr

From the time I received your letter on the 17th, I was exceſſively melancholy, which was much increaſed by your ſilence. But when this was brought me, I could not conceal my grief. I ran into my father's room, and begged he would ſuffer me to go to London, and bring you down with me. He requeſted to be let into the circumſtances; I readily complied with it, as I thought that would be the beſt method of enforcing my plea.

He made anſwer, "he did not know how things were—you might be the artful creature you were repreſented to be—At leaſt it was not proper you ſhould be my companion—He would aſk his wife's advice."

How was I mortified!—he left the room, or my anger would have burſt forth.

My *virtuous* mother-in-law exclaimed againſt you with a moſt virulent modeſty,—"What!" ſaid I, "are you apprehenſive your morals will be contaminated by the converſation of Miſs Melmoth? Admitting ſhe is what her infernal enemies have repreſented her, ſurely you could not fear danger."

I am afraid my zeal did you more miſchief than ſervice—High words were the conſequence: and my cruel father laid ſevere injunctions on my not ſeeing you—I now feel the leſſening my ſtipend. Ah! how I wiſh I was of age, then would I fly to you, and bear you to ſome peaceful retreat—there would my Caroline and her Sidney reſide—the world forgetting and by it forgot—For what happineſs do we reap from ſociety?—

Tho' my father's execration were the conſequence, I will write to you: nothing can or ſhall hinder me.

I could now wiſh I had accepted Mordaunt's offer, then I ſhould have had a houſe to receive my lovely injured friend—But yet do not deſpond, my Caroline: your virtue will one day ſhine out more conſpicuous

conspicuous for the malice which has over-clouded it at present. Mrs. Grafton's eyes may at length be opened. I pity her; she is really an excellent woman—but too apt to be biassed by the artful. Ah! how I feel your pangs of slighted love, and cold disdain!—Foolish, infatuated man---what hast thou lost!

Be not scrupulous, my dearest love, in accepting the inclosed---I have no use for it. I shall think you doubt my affection, if you make any difficulty in taking what is so much your own---for so is, and shall be, every thing which belongs to me. We have but one heart, we will have but one purse. O that we were together! that you might pour forth your sorrows into my bosom---that we might mingle our tears; and that in time I might dispel your griefs---at least, alleviate them by sharing them with you!

Could you for one moment think your Sidney would forsake you? Harbour not such an idea. Think the greatest impossibilities easy to be accomplished ---but never doubt the love, the unalterable love, of

Your

SIDNEY VERE.

LETTER LXIII.

To Miss VERE.

September, 29.

THE greatest consolation a heart like mine could receive, was your dear welcome letter. How could I doubt my Sidney! Ah! how could I doubt

doubt my Darnley! O, my sweet friend---there my heart bleeds——How can I divest myself of these soul-harrowing thoughts? Reputation blasted!—Ruined with the man I adored!—He too to think me guilty!—To cast me from him!—What a trial for me, ever tender and susceptible of sorrow! I marvel my heart is not quite broken.—But I am called away, I know not by whom

In Continuation.

Protect me Heaven! Ah, Sidney, who do you think came to me?—In whose lodgings am I—my God in his! I entered the dining-room, where I heard somebody was, who begged to see me on an affair of consequence Who should I then behold, but the infamous Lord L. I was turning hastily out of the room he stept between me and the door, seized both my hands, and threw himself at my feet I sunk, all pale and trembling, into a chair, and shrieking with terror, strove to disengage my hands from his touch, which was worse than poison to me

He begged forgiveness—I told him on two conditions I would grant it.——" Name them; by Heaven I would forego all other happiness to procure it"

" First, my lord, to leave me—I have no more reputations to lose—no more friends to abandon me: you cannot make me more miserable, therefore can have no business here——The next, go to Mrs Grafton, clear my innocence, confess your motives for engaging in so vile a plot, to ruin me in all my expectations"

" And think you Madam," rising, I have taken all these pains to gain you, and tamely give you up—branding my name with villain!—No, my dear creature, I have won you, and now will wear you"

" Harbour

"Harbour not a surmise of that sort, thou infernal monster, there are powers to whom I c and will apply for protection. I am not the h roine of a novel, my lord, who will quietly be away with, but a free-born English woman, will assert my prerogative. If you do not leave house this instant, I will put myself under the p tection of the Lord Chancellor; he will, I tru not, keep me from falling into the greatest of m series—your hands.—Leave me, my lord, you have no further business with me."

"My dear Caroline, as I said before, I h gone too far to lose you now: be but mine will settle half my estate on you. By Heaven I lo you more than life, and nothing but despair losing you for ever, should have urged me to e cute a plan suggested by Miss Grafton, but w I abhorred; nor would I have consented, had other means of obtaining you presented itself.—L suffer my love and despair, most adorable Carol to plead for me.—Reflect, there was once a ti when you loved *me* ——you certainly merited so punishment for your inconstancy. Consent, love ——It shall be the sole business of my life if you will agree to live with me—to constitute happiness."

"I know not, my lord, whether your stupi or insolence merit my contempt and hatred m I am equally astonished at both. Can you be foolish to imagine, the way to render yourself greeable to a woman of virtue, is to shew yours the vice-gerent of the devil—or have the insolen to suppose any thing you can offer, an atonem for the injuries you have done me? If you wish intitle yourself to my thanks, act the part—diff cult to you—of a man of honor: by that mea only can you make me reparation."

"Pr

"By heaven! were the task an Herculean labour, I would attempt and accomplish it, could I hope you would be my reward—Nay, I would forfeit my life, to conciliate your esteem—I know I have injured you in the eye of the world, in the eye of the world I can make you reparation—Accept my hand and fortune. Had I the world in possession, I would thus, kneeling, lay it at your feet"

—"The world and you I equally despise—What! can you think so poorly of me, as to imagine I would now deign to receive your prostituted vows? I refused your offers when I only thought you an immoral man, dost thou think I would now accept them? No—beggary—nay, eternal infamy would I suffer, rather than give your impious passion the least sanction—I shall take proper methods to prevent ever again being insulted by your odious presence" Saying which, I rang the bell, and Mrs Wilson appeared, I told her in the presence of Lord L "never, on any account, to admit that gentleman again, if she did, she must be answerable for any consequences that might ensue This caution will be necessary only for a few days I shall then have found an asylum, where it will be impossible any one, disagreeable to me, can find me out" I left them immediately, and retired to my closet

The presence of this vile man disconcerted me exceedingly, tho' I think I acted right in not appearing afraid of him it will prevent his taking open measures, and as for secret plots, I shall keep very close, and by that means, frustrate any he may suggest I do not suppose he will run away with me, and lock me up Those incidents are only to be found in romances mine, alas! is a true history, ah! would to heaven it were not! I should weep over such a tale, properly related. In novels,

novels, the heroine is always extricated out of difficulties, while the only release I can expect is death.

* * *

Thank Heaven! Mrs Johnson is arrived. The good woman wept on my neck, as she folded me in her maternal arms, and on her knees implored justice on me and my enemies. She said, she would risk all Miss Grafton's anger, and endeavour to convince her of my innocence. I dissuaded her from so fruitless an attempt, as answering no other purpose than instigating my malicious enemies to injure me yet further, if it proves in their power.

The affection this good woman expresses for me, and the pious consolations she gives me, afford me infinite satisfaction.

Would you think it, the illness of Mrs Johnson's sister was a falsity, propagated by that prince of liars, Lord I—, on purpose to get her out of the way, thinking by that means to distress me still further, rightly judging I should immediately go to her. The next step was to engage one of his agents to take the whole house in his name, tho' that was to be a profound secret to me. Mrs Wilson told Mrs Johnson, "she wondered the young lady could be so hard-hearted to so kind a gentleman; for during her illness, my lord came every two hours to enquire after her health, nay that he often slept in the house, and would let his chariot wait at the door for hours together, in case it was wanted to go for a doctor." By which politic scheme I make no doubt he has effectually blasted my reputation publicly. He made me miserable before, I cannot be more so.

Mrs. Johnson is gone in quest of a lodging for me; I am waiting the success of her embassy.

Nothing

Nothing but the apprehension of offending my dearest Sidney, should have prevailed on me to accept the note Limited as your finances are now, I think I ought not It is an old quotation from Pope, that "man wants but little here below, nor wants that little long" I must endeavour to contract my wants to my circumstances A great sum of money has been expended on my education I had naturally good talents which I have improved The acquiring the knowledge of many things, for which you would sometimes laugh at me, will now be of singular advantage to me What used to employ me for amusement, must now be subservient to a more laudable purpose the procuring means to get an honest livelihood I would rather do that, than seek a precarious one by waiting on any body. besides, who would take me without a character? what would a lady think, were a person of my appearance to apply for the place of an Abigail? I have, I think, too much pride for that station No surely, my knowledge in drawing, painting, tambour, and a variety of other works, may, with œconomy, be sufficient to maintain me in tolerable decency Cloaths, you know, I have enough when altered to last my life—at least I hope so I see nothing on this side eternity to wish to remain here, and though I am forsaken by all the world, Heaven will still behold, and receive me with mercy.

I continually pray to be strengthened, but, alas! my Sidney, it is at present in vain in the midst of my aspirations to the throne of grace, my thoughts wander back to earth, and I wish I was not the wretched thing I feel I am

"To feel, to know myself innocent, is my only support but likewise to know myself an outcast from society, is the constant source of affliction

When I reflect on the happy prospects which once opened to my view, is it to be wondered, that being

being sensible of my afflictions as a mortal, I likewise feel them as a mortal? Can it be a matter of astonishment to any one, that when the domestic occurrences of life subside, the recollection of what I once was, and what I now am, should rush on my tortured imagination, and that I break out into loud lamentations of my cruel destiny? I look in the glass, and then throw myself in a chair, and give vent to my sorrows in a fresh flood of tears. —But I shall afflict my Sidney too much. I shall be easier by-and-by.

* * *

Mrs Johnson is returned. She acquaints me she has seen a lodging, very snug and proper for me, but there is not room for her. I do not like to part with her, tho' I do not know if I may not be more concealed by myself. She can be near me, and with me every day, if I chuse it.—I shall take it on her recommendation.—I enclose a direction. —Let me hear from you very often, and remember it is the only comfort left

Your faithful

CAROLINE MELMOTH.

LETTER LXIV.

To Miss MELMOTH.

Vere-Park, Oct. 2.

OUT of zeal to my beloved Caroline, I have executed a project of my own, which occurred to me immediately on the knowledge of the ... ment unmerited sufferings of my angel-friend It has not had the desired effect, nay, perhaps I may rather have done you disservice, where I meant and strove for your advantage But I know you too well, to believe you will love me the less for my unsuccessful attempt

I was frustrated in my ardent wishes of having you with me—I knew, had I consulted you about the affair in question, you would not have consented, even had the advantages appeared as plainly obvious to you, as I thought they did to me—I was morally certain you would have objected to such a proceeding, from the ineffable goodness of your heart not permitting you to do justice to yourself, by making a full discovery of Miss Grafton's baseness, and having the means in your power, throw the guilt upon the right person—I therefore took that task upon myself I wrote a long letter to Mrs Grafton—I laid before her the injustice she had done the best, the worthiest of her sex warned her not to harbour such a snake in her bosom as the vile Letitia, as I could prove her to be, from several letters of my beloved friend, tho' I was certain you had in tenderness to her (Miss Grafton) suppressed many of her impious crimes, for which she had rewarded you, by basely urging Mrs Grafton to throw from her heart a jewel above price. You know I am very urgent on occasion, I said all that a heart fired with resentment at your unworthy treatment, and glowing with the warmest friendship, could inspire.—I affirmed your total ignorance of my procedure, which I had concealed from you for the above reasons—In short, my letter was long, and filled with the most respectful terms towards Mrs Grafton, tho' I could not restrain my pen when I mentioned her infernal niece

I anticipated the joy I should receive on the advantages which would accrue to my adorable Caroline

line—Nothing but the most perfect reconciliation filled my heart I longed, ardently longed for a return to my epistle at length an answer came—I will transcribe it for you, in my rage I tore the letter thro—O that it had been the writer! Detestable, infamous wretch!

To Miss VERE

Madam,

Waving the many kind and very friendly epithets you honoured me with in your truly polite letter to Mrs Grafton, I proceed to inform you by that lady's request, that she is but too sensible the basen ess of your friend—I will not contaminate my pen by suffering it to write her name—And the intercession of any one in that creature's behalf could have effect, the worthy Miss Sidney Vere would still be unsuccessful—You will pardon freedom in others, since you pique yourself on your freedom of style

I believe it would have been better for the infamous girl to have restrained her licentious principles, at least so far as not to have made me the subject of her friendly correspondence with you What your character may be I know not, but as it is said, we are to judge of people by the company they keep, it must in my mind at best remain doubtful

I suppose I need not tell you, no letter for the future bearing the signature of Vere will be read; they will be burnt on the immediate receipt of them

Yet perhaps, you have been made the dupe of this abandoned wretch, if so, I sincerely pity you she had art to deceive older and wiser people than yourself me she never deceived I knew her long tho' such was my tenderness for her character, I never should have noted her infamous practices, had they not become too flagrant to bear longer concealment, and had not my innocence been as apparent as her guilt was enormous, I should have been involved in the same ruin But you may assure yourself, I am too firmly fixed in my aunt's favour, for any weak efforts of yours, or your *angel-friend* thro' you, to determine You never can or shall gain any advantage over me by your united arts

I must further say, to exculpate the severity with which you may fancy yourself treated by your parents—tho' you will soon have reason to thank both them and me,—that I have, by command of Mrs Grafton, written Lady Vere an account of your audacity and the base infamy of your colleague, together with some of the heads of your letter to my dear aunt, who says, she could readily pardon your intent of deceiving her, but cannot overlook the asperity of your reflections on a niece highly beloved by her You see the basis is too strong for your shallow artifice to sap —It shall be my sole business to conciliate my aunt's affection still more

I have no resentment either to you or your friend, I despise ye both too much —

Yours,

LETITIA GRAFTON.

This letter may serve to shew the power a bad woman may gain over one whose faculties are weakened by age. could she otherwise have assumed such an ascendency over Mrs Grafton? But I beg you, my dearest Caroline, to forgive my ill judged zeal.—I now wish I had consulted you You would

would have seen the affair in its true light, as now appears to me —Might I not suppose the diabolical Miss Grafton would prevent any letter reaching the hand of her aunt without inspection —She certainly suppressed my letter, as it would have raised some doubts at least, in the mind of Mrs Grafton, which perhaps, unprepared, Miss Grafton would have had no subterfuge to evade

I might have foreseen the consequences as they have fallen out, had I been blest with your good sense and penetration, but whenever I take a whim in my head of doing any thing, whether important or trivial, I rush on it headlong, not giving myself time to reflect on the consequences —As the silly young girls say, I believe I was bewitched, and it is done, and cannot be undone —small consolation that, in this and many other cases But however I hope, if I have not been so happy as to succeed in my endeavours for your service, I have not, as Miss Grafton would insinuate, been the means of irritating Mrs Grafton still more against you, and set all prospects of a happy reconciliation at a farther distance

Well, you have seen but one effect of my misguided zeal a letter was received at the same time by Lady Vere, as was threatened, which now [illegible] spirit to revile my lovely friend, nor did I escape without my share My father [illegible] us with his blessed comparison, and I was [illegible] a full tedious hour, with odious repetition Don't think I was silent all this while no, no made my precious mamma look horridly blank several times, I assure you, and when she had vented all her spleen, and was incapable of answering a few questions I put to her, with some degree of ceremony and more truth, she burst forth in a most copious flood of tears, of which she has always a reservoir very near her eyes, and which a called in as auxiliary forces when ſhe ſees occaſion. She had then abſolute need of them, for my father, which perhaps you will ſcarcely believe, began to liſten to reaſon, tho' flowing from the lips of his daughter; therefore, had not her ladyſhip's allies, before recorded, came up to her aſſiſtance, I might have remained maſter, or rather miſtreſs of the field.—But it was not in nature to ſupport ſuch a ſight,—to behold her lovely eyes ſuffuſed in tears, —and all for my good too,—"For what advantage, my deareſt Sir William, can the diſgrace of the vile Miſs Melmoth be of to me, you know! I am ſure, the connection which your daughter has with her makes me tremble, leſt ſhe ſhould avail herſelf of her power over our dear Sidney, and draw her in to countenance her vices—ſuch an event would be bringing down both of us with ſorrow to our graves.—But Sidney looks upon me as her enemy."—I could not ſtay to hear her hypocriſy, therefore left Sir William to the taſk of conſoling his virtuous wife, and my no-leſs careful ſtep-mother.

In conſequence of the conſultation of the danger which may reſult to their beloved daughter, a third abridgment is made of my allowance, ſo that from two hundered *per-annum*, I am now reduced to ſixty.—How do I now repent the ſums I fooliſhly ſquandered away! Tho' no money I ever ſpent gave me uneaſineſs 'till now, except what I gave to Miſs Arnold: in order to ſave her delicacy a bluſh, I pretended it as a loan, but her ladyſhip does not think it incumbent on her to pay the debts contracted by Miſs Arnold.

But I can find ways and means to raiſe ſupplies: I can never be in the leaſt difficulty, nor ſhall you; I will never forgive you, if you are obliged to have recourſe to any one, myſelf excepted.—I can borrow.—Lady Betty Crauford will make no objection to become my creditor.—When I come of age, my

plan

plan is fixed —I will not urge your quitting Lon- don, as I find you are kept there almost invol- tarily—you are impelled to continue there by over-ruling impulse—I know not how to blame you in your case, I should not act with half your [illegible] dence, but no one would expect it of me —A[illegible] my best beloved —

SIDNEY VE[illegible]

LETTER LXV

To Miss VERL.

Oct. [illegible]

MY most grateful thanks are due to my [illegible] all hopes of forgiveness from my [illegible] respectable Mrs Grafton are vain I cease to [illegible] dulge them —Ah! could I divest myself of all ot[illegible] hopes, as vain! as fruitless! weak as the "ba[illegible] fabric of a vision"

I certainly should have made some objection [illegible] any intercession, as I promised my late patrone[illegible] would never make the least, until there was a pro- bability of clearing my innocence to her —I kno[illegible] it would be in vain —but my obligation to you still the same Why was you born with a heart formed for friendship? Or why rather did you [illegible] bestow your love on some one happier than I —Why, one marked out by Heaven and all [illegible] to tread the paths of misery? Why must I gi[illegible] pain to those, I would die to relieve?—

I might lead a dull contented life, could I ro[illegible] from remembrance my lost scenes of happiness

Cou[illegible]

Could I forget
What I have been, I might the better bear
What I am destin'd to I'm not the first
That have been wretched but to think how much
I have been happier

Could I forget the amiable qualities of the most amiable of men, I could support my own misfortunes with the stoicism of a Philosopher, but he —the man my soul rested on—he to believe me infamous! he, who fondly gazed on me, to throw me from him, "like a detested sin,"—'tis there —'tis there I bleed —

But ah! my sweet friend, I am the unhappy cause of dissensions in your family Do not, do not, my best love, for your Caroline's sake, give way to your too great vivacity in these altercations Consider, your father knows not every circumstance of my eventful life as you do I am looked on as an out-cast by all the world, I have no friend on earth but yourself, ah! do not urge me to say, I am sorry you love me so well since, in your affection to a wretch abandoned of all, you forget your duty, so indispensable to your parent —Let this have weight with my beloved friend

I like the lodgings I am settled in very well they are small, but commodious —Mrs Johnson is almost continually with me, and contributes to my resignation by her pious example I think I am singularly fortunate in meeting with such a comforter in my distress.

Poor woman, she has suffered many calamities I had promised myself great felicity, if I could have done it without disobliging Miss Grafton, to have taken her to live with me as a superintendant of the family—or at least to have settled something on her, to enable her to live comfortably · these,

 my

my dear, were my intentions, had it pleased H ven to have blest me, with all my heart wis for here below But it is over, Sidney! "Not but despair my fancy paints, no dawn of hope I s —I must emulate Mrs Johnson's example, seek happiness and comfort only from Heav there must my treasure be My enemy cannot br through, and rob me of eternal bliss

After some inquiry, Mrs Johnson has met w a milliner, Stevens her name, to whom I can pose of some trifles I have long possessed

My chief avocation will be the *broder au tam* You used to say, I worked too quick at it fo gentlewoman, I shall now reap the advantage my avidity in that fashionable branch of fem education —I am finishing a waistcoat, begun another purpose, like that I worked for you w at Vere-park Ah! what floods of tears have I sh over it! How does the most trifling incident b back to my tortured memory, scenes which are ever fled! Oh that all traces were obliterated fr my mind!

I have finished several things, tho' the waist has been in hand the whole time But it is v seldom I can form resolution to make any progr in it. when my mind is more strengthened, I sh pursue it with industry

Mrs Stevens has seen it, and was profuse in commendations, begged to know, if I meant dispose of it, as she would give me any price for her question brought the tears in my eyes, wh I endeavoured to conceal, she saw my emoti but politely took no notice of it, and turned discourse —I took occasion to give her a ficti account of myself, lest she should imagine th was some mystery in my history, and take so method I might not chuse to satisfy her curiosi I therefore hinted the fault of parents, in educati

th

their children above their worldly abilities, breeding them up to be gentlewomen, with little to support that station, as must be the case where an income is precarious, and held by no other tenure than a man's life—Saying I thought I was very fortunate in meeting with her, who appeared a woman of worth and character, as I was a stranger to London, &c —All which I perceived Mrs Stevens readily gave me credit for —Innocent, and in itself laudable, as this deception is, yet my heart detests it Ah! Sidney, why am I compelled to conceal the sentiments of a heart which delights in sincerity? —To what dreadful resources am I driven by my cruel enemies!

"Adieu, love me always, it is my only support

CAROLINE MELMOTH

LETTER LXVI

To EDWARD GRENVILLE, Esq.

Bruton-street, October 10

NO, Grenville, I cannot yet believe the lovely Miss Melmoth is guilty——at least in so high a degree as she has been represented

I hastened to town on the receipt of your alarming letter —how is my heart still interested in the fate of that charming woman! Ah! had you seen her when first I disclosed my passion to her—But the scene is too tender—the repetition would soften me too much

I went to Mrs. Grafton's house, and was intro-

duced to her niece—After a few common pla
compliments, equally inſincere on both ſide,
begged I might have the honor of ſeeing M
Grafton—She heſitated—I repeated my requeſt
adding, "you muſt give me leave to inform th
lady, I wiſh much to ſee her."—I rang the be
—A ſervant appeared—"Tell my aunt, Sir Jo
Evelin is here"—"And earneſtly begs to be adm
ted," interrupted I, "to her preſence" Miſs Gr
ton ſeemed unwilling that I ſhould, and by wa
preventing me, ſaid, "her aunt's ſpirits were v
low, and deſired I would be careful not to men
the name of the infamous wretch who had been
occaſion of it"

"I am a ſtranger to your meaning, Madam

"Surely, Sir John, you muſt have heard
the creature's being detected?"

"I wiſh her enemies were," ſaid I, fixing
eyes upon Miſs Grafton

"I thought, Sir John, you had been too g
a young man to countenance vice"

"I hope I am, Madam—and therefore m
that wiſh"

"I do not underſtand *you* now"

"I believe you do," I anſwered with a
ſmile Mrs Grafton, coming into the room, p
vented an anſwer, which, by Miſs Grafton's lo
would have been, I believe, full of acrimony

I was determined, notwithſtanding Miſs Graf
admonition, to enter on the topic my heart
filled with directly

"I am extremely ſorry to find you ſo indiſpo
Madam, ſtill more ſo for the occaſion"

"Ah! Sir John," lifting up one of her ha
"indiſpoſed indeed, how can I be otherw
Indeed, indeed, I did not merit ſuch a return"
The tears gliſtered in her venerable eyes

"I cannot believe the unhappy Miſs Melm

is so guilty as you, Madam, have been induced to think her."

"O Sir John, it was not 'till the fullest conviction of her baseness I discharged her.—Can any one think for a trifling offence I would have shut my doors against one I had cherished so long?—No. She is the most abandoned of women.—She behaved so as not to have one friend left."

"None that can gain admittance to you, Madam, I readily believe.—That Miss Melmoth has enemies I am not now to learn, but who were they? Those whose interest it was to be so."

"Upon my word, Sir John, Miss Melmoth is much obliged to you."

"I wish, Madam, she had the same obligation to you."

"Could any one speak in her favor," said Mrs Grafton, "I should be too willing to hear them—but that is impossible.—She has lived ever since with her infamous choice."

"Alas! where—to whom was she to fly? If an unhappy woman makes a false step—unless she has great art indeed—she must still persist.—Ah! Madam, would it not, admitting she had deviated from the path of virtue, would it not have been the better way—worthy your goodness, to endeavour to save her from deeper guilt?"

"Sir John, you can say nothing in her defence. I would have preserved her from continuing in her wicked course, had she been retrievable.—My resentment subsided with the approaching morning, I sent her a proposal, calculated for her advantage—but she ever refused my bounty. Would she have done that, unless she had been secure of a settlement from her seducer?"

"Well do you stile him seducer—He must have used uncommon art indeed, to tempt a woman of her sentiment, to embrace certain infamy.—But pardon me, Madam, if I still doubt."

"You are to judge as you please, Sir John, I have acted so Yet how much has this event c[illegible] me! But it is a subject I cannot dwell upon I feel too much!—Could I have seen the least pen[illegible] tence—had she made the least overtures—but n[illegible] she was incorrigible---The dread of meeting h[illegible] any where, keeps me a prisoner in my own hou[illegible] ---Ah! could I support the beholding her in t[illegible] situation she has chosen!---she whom I held nea[illegible] my heart---even to the prejudice of my niece- I have too long been negligent of her merit."

As I found there was little appearance of my be[illegible] of service to poor Miss Melmoth, and that I w[illegible] rather an unwelcome visitant---I took my leave

I know not what to think of this affair---It certain, she was above a fortnight at lodgings hir[illegible] for her reception by Lord L. 'tis as certain she a[illegible] companied him to Paris---These at least are t[illegible] reports---Yet still, when I reflect on all her beh[illegible] viour---her modest diffidence---her sense---no, cannot be---O that I could find her out---discov[illegible] her retreat! And must a lovely woman for one fal[illegible] step be driven from society, and be branded wi[illegible] infamy, while the wretch, who betrays the fo[illegible] believing creature, triumphs in his guilt? Ah! ho[illegible] unequal the dispensations of man!---I blush, that am one of the sex

The defection from virtue in the fair, tho' one which will admit of many palliating circum[illegible] stances, is nevertheless the most punished by th[illegible] own sex. How ready is every woman, whose vi[illegible] tue was never put to the proof, or whose co[illegible] stitution is restrained by apathy, to join the com[illegible] mon cry, and hunt the stricken deer to destruction If in one soft moment, from placing too great confidence in her lover's *honor*, she loses her *ow[illegible]* a whole life of penitence and tears can never, the eye of the world, waſh away her guilt—No not that ſincere repentance, which is promiſed by our creator to make us as white as ſnow, tho' we were by our ſins as red as ſcarlet, can meet forgiveneſs from thoſe whom it is impoſſible ſhe can have offended—unleſs they imagine, from her fall, the virtue of her ſex is called in queſtion. The ladies never reflect on the body of men, becauſe ſome have proved villains, and ſuffered puniſhment by the laws. Nor is a man, known to be a villain, treated by moſt of them with the ſcorn he merits.

As a learned writer ſays; let every woman deteſt vice in herſelf, but let her not, by her outrageous perſecution of it in others, give room for ſuſpicions greatly to her diſadvantage.—Miſs Grafton, who with ſuch over-virtuous fury exclaims againſt the unhappy Caroline, has, I believe, much of the guilt in this affair to anſwer for.—You know my ſentiments of her, and likewiſe thoſe of her amiable brother, which however he never willingly diſcloſes.—She was always artful and deſigning.—She has had the addreſs to turn every thing to her own advantage. I once mentioned to you my ſuſpicions of her deſigns upon me. Once I was alone with her ſome hours—I am not a vain man, but ſhe made me ſuch advances, as many men of leſs ſentiment would have taken advantage of. I confeſs I feel great lenity to the failings of the fair, that proceed from the tender paſſions, but I am not one who would ever ſolicit, or even accept, the favors of a woman, who has a reputation to loſe.

Adieu, my friend, believe me

Yours ſincerely,

JOHN EVELIN

The lady's ſituation continuing the ſame, many letters for brevity-ſake are omitted.

LETTER LXVII

To Miſs VERE.

February 5

I Went this morning, according to my uſu[al] cuſtom, to Mrs Stevens when I entered [the] ſhop, I ſaw there a lady ſeemingly about fifty, wh[o] was admiring the waiſtcoat I had ſome time befo[re] ſent thither to be diſpoſed of She ſaid a gre[at] deal in praiſe of the deſign and workmanſhip, a[nd] applying to me, aſked my opinion of it the que[s]tion diſconcerted me extremely, I anſwered, "[I] could not look on myſelf as a judge." "You [are] the propereſt perſon," ſaid the abrupt Mrs. Ste[] vens, "to pronounce its merit, ſince you plann[ed] and executed it yourſelf" "Good God!" ex[] claimed the ſtrange lady, "Is this the young la[dy] of whom you gave me ſome account? O Mrs. Ste[] vens, how blind is the world to real merit, if it ca[n] ſuffer this amiable young creature to experien[ce] any other than its ſmiles!"

"Alas! madam," ſaid I, "my caſe is not ſin[] gular, I make no doubt there are many infinite[ly] more deſerving than myſelf, who have met w[ith] the ſame misfortunes Nor indeed have I ſo muc[h] to complain of, I have health, and only myſelf [to] maintain That piece which you are ſo obliging [to] commend ſo much, was the produce of my idl[e] hours I little thought then I ſhould have had occ[a]ſion to part with it for the neceſſaries of life!" "Nor ſhall you part with it, my ſweet girl," ſaid the lady "I have taken a great fancy to you and if you will make me happy in your compan[y] it is all the return I will aſk for what I intend do[ing] for you.—Mrs Stevens, I cannot forgive you fo[r] not bringing me before acquainted with this excel[] lence

Your parents, my dear, I hear are dead. —What an allay of happineſs, does Heaven permit the departed to be ſenſible of the tranſactions of mortals, to ſee a darling child, nurtured with the tendereſt care, obliged to ſeek a precarious living from a world which ought to afford her nothing but delights! I am not young, as you may ſee, I am older in my ſentiments and manner of life than in years. You ſeem to have a ſerious turn. If you can like the company of a woman, ſuch as you ſee me, I have a houſe, a heart, a purſe, all diſpoſed to admit you a ſharer.—I have long, as Mrs Stevens knows, been ſeeking an amiable ſenſible companion of my own ſex, ſuch, if I have any ſkill in phiſiognomy, you are."

Do not think, my dear Sidney, I was ſilent all this time: no, I made my proper acknowledgments for her kindneſs.---My unhappy warfare thro' life has, I am afraid, weakened that general philanthropy I uſed to feel. I could not help thinking this ſtranger's generoſity carried too far.---How liable muſt ſuch a woman be to be deceived! how very few the inſtances of any one being ſo ſuddenly attached, and ſo liberal of their purſe and protection!---After expreſſing my gratitude, which ſhe would hardly permit, "I told her, I had received an offer from a friend of my father's to reſide in the country, and muſt give her an anſwer. I was apprehenſive I ſhould not find it ſo agreeable as the ſcheme now propoſed, but politeneſs demanded I ſhould at leaſt pay ſome attention to it."---

She ſeemed hardly ſatisfied at my reply, ſhe wanted to take me home with her directly, but made me promiſe to meet her the next day at Mrs Stevens's and accompany her home. Mrs Stevens inſiſted that we ſhould both dine with her on the morrow.---Mrs Henley, for that I found was her name, agreed to the propoſal, and undertook to anſwer for her lovely young friend, ſo ſhe was pleased to style me ---" My dear," said she, "we will take an airing to-morrow morning, when I hope we shall settle all preliminaries, in the mean time I would have you discharge your lodgings, for which I must intreat your acceptance of this note"---This, you my believe, I peremptorily refused, tho' with politeness—I smiled, and told her, "I could not suffer her to confer favors of that sort 'till she was convinced I was worthy such bounty" "She begged my pardon, declared she had not the least intention of wounding my delicacy—She considered riches as of no further use than to bestow, where Heaven had given every other requisite in life, but that which the misjudging world held in too high estimation"

* * *

Upon reflection, I do not well know what to make of this adventure—Would to Heaven I could be informed by intuition of your sentiments concerning it It certainly, in my opinion—at least I used to think so—argues a bad heart to be ever suspicious, and imagine no one can perform a generous action without a sinister view in it.—Surely I ought not of all persons to give way to unjust suspicion, since I have received proofs both in the revered Mr Melmoth, and my dear Mrs. Grafton, that truly noble and generous persons seek their reward in their own hearts; what other could they expect to reap from their unexampled tenderness to a poor deserted orphan, but the ineffable delight proceeding from the heart-felt satisfaction of doing a virtuous action? I fear, my beloved Sidney, my heart is not right—not as it used to be—else why this curiosity, if I may so term it, to find out the real motive of Mrs Henley's generosity? I cannot persuade myself but there is some hidden

hidden one—Mrs Johnſon is not in town, ſhe went yeſterday to her ſiſter's at St Albans; ſhe returns to morrow I wiſh ſhe was here to conſult with, but I am predetermined not to go to this offered aſylum, 'till I have both her's and your advice upon it—Adieu, my deareſt love—I will not cloſe this letter 'till I have ſeen more of my new acquaintance—

February 6

Sidney, I had certainly a *preſſentiment*, that this good lady and I ſhould not make agreeable companions—And yet, to do her juſtice, it is not her fault, for I dare ſay ſhe would gladly receive me into her houſe.—Once I was in it—I little thought Mrs Henley the miſtreſs of it—Ah! my God! from that fatal evening may I date all my miſery!—Why are theſe ſcenes recalled to my memory?—Why are the newly cloſed wounds burſt open afreſh?—But do not let me anticipate.—You are doubtleſs all impatience,—thus then I endeavour to ſatisfy it.

At eleven this morning I went to Mrs Stevens, who informed me Mrs Henley had been waiting ſome time for me, and was impatient to ſee me.—As ſhe led me up ſtairs, ſhe was profuſe in her praiſes of the goodneſs and beneficence of her gueſt's heart, congratulating me on the ſtate of affluence and caſe I ſhould ſhare with Mrs Henley—This from any other I ſhould have received with more pleaſure, but, as I once hinted, I did not much like Mrs Stevens, not having reaſon to believe ſhe would be very delicate if encouraged to the contrary—She once ſaid, ſhe was for enjoying life, nor could ſhe think, while a woman was in the height of youth and beauty, any purchaſe could be too dear—I took the liberty of ſhewing my diſapprobation of her aſſertion, I had the argument on my ſide, and I ſpoke with energy.

ergy—Mrs Henley commended my obfervations and reflections, "declaring fhe never met with any body with fuch exalted fentiments, what an ineftimable treafure fhe would have in me!" By the bye, I thought fhe had not kept very good company, if my remarks, which were trite, and I think common to every virtuous breaft, appeared fo extremely fingular—Yet really there was nothing exceptionable in her manner, tho' I could not feel a mutual flame, or that our fouls were congenial, as fhe feveral times faid they were

When we had taken fome chocolate, we prepared for our airing—I would fain have excufed myfalf from dining with them, faying, I had letters to write, and likewife appointed to meet fomebody in the evening—Mrs Stevens politely faid, fhe would not detain me longer in the afternoon than was agreeable, but that Mrs Henley would be quite unhappy, if I deprived them of my company till the laft moment Mrs. Henley faid a thoufand obliging things

"Do my dear," continued fhe, "get a releafe from your father's friend as foon as poffible, I cannot live without you—You muft fpend all to morrow with me"

"I affured her, I would if poffible, as I fhould be happy in affording her every inftance of my gratitude"

"That's my fweet creature," returned fhe—Turning to Mrs Stevens, "Ah! what havock, I warrant, has that lovely face made among the country beaux!—What eyes—what a complexion!"—I could not help fmiling at the old lady's rapture—"Heavens!" fhe continued, what a fmile!—You was formed to infpire all hearts with love—That fmile would humanize a favage but I beg your pardon---I make you blufh ---I am a very great admirer of beauty in my own fex, and no bad judge" "No wonder, madam," I replied, "since you must have laid claim to a great share a few years ago"

"O fye, you little flatterer," returned she, tapping my cheek, "you must not talk thus to an old woman"

The coach being ready, we stepped into it and took an air thro' Hyde-Park, returning the back-way---Mrs Henley recollected something she wanted at home, and ordered the coach to come round by Bloomsbury---We stopped at a large house, which I thought bore some resemblance to the fatal one, whither I was decoyed by the crafty wiles of Miss Grafton---The servant was going to open the door, but Mrs Henley said there was no need, only she wanted to speak to her woman The woman appearing, she said something to her in a low voice---Mrs Henley asked her, if any one had called. Yes, the servant answered, Colonel Clayton was at that time in the house.---On a stricter scrutiny, I was confirmed in my suspicion of the house being the same, but if any doubt remained, the appearance of Colonel Clayton obviated it. Think what was my confusion, when I beheld the companion of Campbell! Good God, what was my situation! The pretended good Mrs Henley, a vile procuress!—I applied my handkerchief to my face, to conceal it from his view, as well as to prevent the strong emotions of my soul from appearing I plainly discovered from the slight glance he caught of my face, that he recollected me: a crowd of horrid ideas presented themselves to my frighted imagination, and nothing but the dread of being carried into that hated house, could have prevented me from fainting

"Surely that face is no stranger to me!" said the Colonel, attempting to take my hand.—"Peace, peace," said Mrs Henley, "this lady is an an intire stranger to you and your rude ways." She whispered something to him, "I beg your pardon, madam," said he, I find I am mistaken. I hope my aunt will say something by way of excusing her mad nephew. You will, madam, to Mrs Henley, engage the lady to sup with you to night, when I hope to be so happy as to make my apologies acceptable." He waited not for my answer, nor indeed was I able then to make one, my unexpected rencontre with him having thrown me into a profound reverie.

The old lady was very elaborate in the praises of her nephew,—tho' the relationship, I suppose, might have been traced up to Adam,—to which however I paid little attention, but observed all she said was echoed by Mrs Stevens.—Well, to shorten the disagreeable occurrences of the day, we dined, and I rose to go home, but found myself constrained to promise that I would return with Mrs Henley to sup, and also to sleep at her house.—Thus was the arch-deceiver foiled at her own weapons, she implicitly believed I would return, because she ardently wished I should.—

As soon as I got home, I took up my pen to give you the promised account.—The woman of the house brought me a letter, which a porter had left. I hastily opened it, a stranger to the hand writing and name, but judge of my astonishment, when I read—

To Miss MIDDLETON.

Madam,

You will no doubt be under some surprise, on receiving so long a letter from one to whom you are quite a stranger. I am the young woman who works in Mrs Stevens's shop, and have had an opportunity

opportunity of seeing, admiring, and I hope (under Heaven) saving you from ruin for such, madam, is intended you, unless this caution, and the good sense beaming in your countenance, have power to save you from the craft of the worst of women

I am sensible I should gain but little credit from many people by what I am going to unfold, but of you, madam, I have a different opinion —My person, if you at all recollect it, is not such as generally covers a vain heart, I can have no other view than protecting innocence from the most diabolical snare ever formed for the destruction of it ---Would to Heaven I had had an adviser---but then, madam, you would not have met with one in me.

I have trod the paths of vice, but never found them flowery, yet they have planted thorns in my breast never to be eradicated by time

It will be necessary to give you some account of my life and misfortunes, that you may be the better judge of your own danger, and learn from my fall to avoid certain misery and guilt, which must be your portion, if ever you set your foot in the house of Mrs. Henley Many have entered it innocent and virtuous, but never was there one returned till they were forced, from crime to crime, to the most abandoned life.

I was daughter to a clergyman, whose living was very small, but was continually in hopes of an increase, till death put an end to his expectations in this life, and my prospects. I had an aunt in London, to whom I wrote an account of my situation, she answered my letter with great tenderness, and desired I would, as soon as possible, settle my affairs and come to town, where she would receive me as a relation to one she dearly loved I joyfully accepted her invitation, and in about six weeks packed up my cloaths, which, with a few pounds,

were

were all my worldly possessions, and arrived in town at my aunt's house --- The servants told me, their mistress had been seized two days before with a fit of apoplexy, in which she died thus was I a second time left destitute,—without friends,—and in a place wholly strange to me The heir of my deceased aunt [she had made no will] told me, I was welcome to remain there some time, till I could hear of something to my advantage I was constrained to accept his offer, but expressed my strong desire of being placed with some milliner he recommended me to Mrs. Stevens; would to heaven I had died the instant I approached her door! then had I been an innocent offering to my Maker I was then very young, and thought handsome—Bred up in the country with the best of fathers, I had no suspicion that youth and beauty excited any other sentiments than tenderness and esteem, at least in my own sex

As soon as Mrs Stevens saw me, she made a bargain, and I was to come directly to her house When I had been with her some little time, she said, perhaps I might like to have some money before the first quarter was expired, she pressed it so much, that at last I accepted the quarterage, giving her a note for it —little did I then think, I was setting fire to a train which was laid to destroy all my future hopes

Mrs Stevens continued to treat me with great civility, but her conversation gave me such offence and uneasiness, as she betrayed too little regard for decency of carriage and virtue, which she laughed at, as very seldom being more than a shadow, and where it was a substance, merely ridiculous —I took every opportunity of letting her see my sentiments differed greatly from her's, and these topics did oft engross our conversations.

Mrs. Henley

Mrs. Henley was very often our visitant, being, as she said, greatly taken with me One day, on Mrs Stevens's leaving the room, after she had with her usual freedom delivered her licentious opinions, Mrs Henley blamed her exceedingly, and told me, she was certain mine could not be an agreeable life, as I was constrained to bear the discourse of one so opposite to myself I have a regard, continued she, for Mrs Stevens, but at the same time condemn her for so freely talking against the reality of virtue, the more so, as I believe there are few women who have gone through life with a fairer character yet, if we are to form a judgment of people, by what they themselves advance in conversation, we should not scruple to pronounce her a bad person But notwithstanding I know Mrs. Stevens to be a woman of strict virtue, I can see she is not agreeable to you if therefore you will come and live with me, by way of companion, I shall be very happy, and will do all in my power to make you so.

It is not material, madam, to give you the particulars of our conference,—suffice it to say, every thing being agreed on, I went joyfully to Mrs Henley's She shewed a great affection for me, was continually making me presents, and insisted on my going to her mercer's, and buying Cloaths, in order to appear as her niece, for such she called me, and repeatedly told me, I should find myself so in her will

But in about a week I found she had other designs, and the horror of my situation stared me in the face. I reproached her with her perfidy, but the cruel monster only laughed at me. In vain did she practise various wiles, in order to bring me to her base designs I firmly told her, I would die first and when I found there were no possible means of escaping, I was determined to put a period

to

to my exiſtence, on which ſhe ſet a watch to prevent me; and one day aſked me whether I would dreſs and ſee company, that being their term to expreſs the moſt horrid meaning I ſtill perſiſted in my refuſal, "Oh! oh!" ſaid ſhe, "I warrant I ſhall find ſome method to bring down your proud ſpirit Do you know this hand-writing?" at the ſame time ſhewing me a note, due from me to Mrs Stevens, for twenty pounds, which ſhe had made over to Mrs Henley, beſides a mercer's bill, board, lodging, &c I thought I ſhould have ſunk with terror —The note was ſigned by me, which I could not deny, though the ſum received was but five pounds, inſtead of twenty. To increaſe my miſery, two dreadful fellows came into the room, and aſked which was their priſoner I threw myſelf at the feet of my betrayer, but ſhe made no other anſwer to my intreaties, than to tell me, unleſs I would comply, a priſon muſt be my portion I aroſe, when I found her inflexible, and put myſelf into the hands of the bailiffs She repreſented my ſteady adherence to virtue, as folly and obſtinacy! Her arguments had no effect on me, and I was hurried to priſon But how ſhall I paint the horrid ſcene which preſented itſelf to my view? It is impoſſible to give you an adequate idea of the horror of Newgate for being deſtitute of money, I was put on the common ſide · there expoſed to the inſults of the moſt abandoned wretches, uttering horrid blaſphemies, and committing every ſpecies of vice that can enter the minds of human beings devoid of all ſenſe of religion or virtue Shocking as my condition was, I yet bore it ſome time, till the ſcanty proviſion, made by the gaol-allowance, and the many miſeries I endured, rendered me wholly inſenſible to every call of virtue.

When the unheard of ills I daily suffered were opposed to the scene Mrs Henley had painted, I was staggered, I knew not on what to determine. Well does Addison say, the woman, who deliberates, is lost, for I too soon consented to leave my prison, and follow my abandoned guide.

As soon as my cheeks regained their usual colour, I was to entertain a gentleman, to whom, my tormentor said, she had great obligations, and as I was a favorite, she deputed me to make him a return. I was under the necessity of seeing him; but had planned a scheme, which I thought could not fail, of throwing myself at his feet, and imploring his pity and protection. I made not the lest doubt of success.——Alas! I then knew not the depravity of human nature, which I have since experienced. With these flattering prospects, I dressed myself to wait on this gentleman, whom Mrs Henley assured me was a man of honor. I had not then learnt, that a man of honor is one capable of the vilest actions, to gratify his base passions

When I found myself alone with this man of honor, he proceeded to take some liberties with me, which, tho' I could expect no less, shocked me excessively; and bursting into tears, at his feet I implored his compassion, in behalf of an innocent young creature, who, unless he had the mercy and compassion to stand her friend, had not one in the world My prayers were rendered useless, could I have hoped to succeed, by the infernal Henley entering the room, in the utmost fury, upbraiding me with deceiving her, and him with want of spirit in losing such an opportunty with so fine a girl; and inhumanly enumerating my charms, in order to stimulate him Suffer me to pass over the guilty scene—From that fatal hour I was lost.

Abandoned to misery and prostitution, my heart felt and acknowledged the force of virtue but how could

could I extricate myself from the labyrinth of vice, into which I had been dragged? Her bond still in force—my reputation blasted—without friends or money to procure them—O how painful! how much worse than the most abject state of labour is the life I then led! condemned to entertain the most infamous of wretches, and to appear gay and lively, when the soul detests the one, and from the unhappy situation, is incapable of the other. Cruel, hard fate!

Tho' I was as far engaged in their vile course of life as I could be, yet the spark of virtue which remained in my bosom, spread itself on my countenance, and I still preserved the semblance of innocence and modesty. This appearance—polluted as I was, dare I call it reality?—was of infinite advantage to Mrs Henley, and she often commended me for it, saying all her girls too soon divested themselves of that charm to the men; for none are so abandoned themselves, as not to admire a modest carriage in others.

I followed this guilty course of life many months, and was the reigning favorite, which Mrs Henley ascribed to my innocent looks, which still bore the appearance of novelty, as if every man was willing to believe that he had been in some measure instrumental in destroying it.

The gentlemen made me presents, which Mrs Henley appropriated to her own use, for she was of opinion, could I have laid by a trifling sum, which might have enabled me to procure any means of subsistence, I would escape from her, as she plainly saw I was far from being reconciled to my way of life.

While in the meridian of my glory, as Mrs Henley used to call it, I was seized with the small-pox, which proved of the worst kind. My terrors on the apprehension of my approaching dissolution, gave me incon-

inconceivable horror, but Mrs Henley, to do her justice, behaved with tenderness during my illness; and when I was recovering, said to me, "You are sensible, Maria, that you can be of no further use to me, your beauty being totally effaced but in consideration of the emolument I have reaped from you, I will never desert you Mrs Stevens cannot refuse taking you into a small share of her business, as she is under obligations to me! Do not therefore despair, you will be well provided for" I thanked her, and accepted of her proposal, and from experience can assure you, that if you go to Mrs Henley's, no human means can extricate you from the snares that are laid to entrap you

If this warning does preserve your innocence, I shall hope my good intention will be accepted by Heaven, as some extenuation of my guilt but, alas! I fear no penitence can restore peace to my wounded mind

I am, Madam,

with the highest regard,

your humble servant,

MARIA CHALMERS.

Ah! my beloved Sidney, what infinite obligations am I under to this unfortunate young woman! What horrid monsters are in the world! Confirmed before in my opinion, I certainly should not have gone back to Mrs Stevens, but by this warning, I am put on my guard Heaven shield me! I will change my lodging, in order to avoid these base women

I wrote

I wrote to the vile old wretch, to excuse my absenting myself, telling her, the relation I spoke of was come to town, &c Adieu, pray for

Your

CAROLINE MELMOTH

LETTER LXVIII

To Mrs JOHNSON

Vere-Park, Feb 21

O! Mrs Johnson, what is become of my beloved friend? A whole fortnight elapsed,—and not a line I scarce know what I write—I am distracted I conjure you let me hear immediately Good God, a whole fortnight! She bade me pray for her —Surely, surely, the vile Henley —O that I could fly to London and share her destiny! If those infernal wretches should have ensnared her,—if—I know not what I would say ——O my good Mrs Johnson you know not,—and yet knowing her so well, you must know how deservedly she is dear to me —Let me, if you have any compassion, let me know all you can learn of her —My whole fortune shall go to save her ——Ah, my God, from what? I send this by a messenger who will bring me your answer, almighty heaven grant happiness to my Caroline whatever becomes of her

SIDNEY VERE

LET-

LETTER LXIX

To Miss Vere

London, Febuary 22

My good lady,

DO not be alarmed, I hope there will not be occasion; and yet,—O Miss Vere! were you to behold me at this instant—I cannot go on—

Best and most amiable of women, what a fate is thine! I bade you not, dear madam, be alarmed, but Oh I fear there is too much reason. My spirits are so much agitated, I can hardly give you all I know of poor Miss Melmoth's situation but be satisfied, she is with me in this house The true cause which has reduced her to this condition, I am yet wholly a stranger to, the effects, I dare not conceal them from you, are dangerous

I was so happy as to rescue her from, what had to me the appearance of imminent danger: a vile wretch would have availed himself of an accident, which threw my dear Miss Melmoth into his protection The frequent fits she afterwards fell into, prevented my receiving any information from herself, nor have I been able to gain any from other people.

A violent fever was brought on by the perturbations of her mind A constant delirium—Oh my good young lady, think what I suffer? Let your generous heart tell you my grief,—to see the dear child, fondly cherished by me in its infancy—Yet I had hopes time might have restored her to the esteem of the world—that the knowledge of her inestimable worth might be owned—But to see this fair flower cropt in its early bloom,—Oh! it is is too much for my aged heart, it will—it will ha- vert—I cannot contain myself,—she will,—she must die, there are no hopes——O, Miss Vere, may heaven,—that heaven which has poured affictions on the dear unhappy Miss Melmoth, be your comforter—my only consolation is that, in the natural course of time, and this last, and severest blow I ever felt, the awful scene must close,

I am, my dear good lady,

Your obliged humble servant,

M JOHNSON

LETTER LXX

To Miss VERE

March,

SUpported in the bed of sickness I dedicate a few, ah! may they be the last, lines to my ever loved Sidney. Just to tell her the earth still bears the wretched Caroline—Mrs Johnson tells me she dispatched an express to you, to inform you of an appearance of my amendment—Worthy woman! How great has been her care, do you my dear, my only friend reward her—She flatters herself I shall recover—Can she wish it? Forgive me, heaven, that I do not—I feel my dissolution approaching. Receive consolation, my inestimable friend, in the close of my afflictions—Think sometimes on her, who till the last moment of life will not cease to love you—Ah, my Sidney! repine not I am thus

thus early cut off, but rejoice that I am so soon released—I am very faint.—Adieu, dearest, best of friends.——

March 2,—

I thought I had taken my last farewel, yet still I exist It was only a fainting fit Mrs Johnson has intreated me not to do any thing which may fatigue me. "Oh! that I could shuffle off this mortal evil"

If ever I shall be able, I will acquaint you with the last sad cause—I must not now think of it: if it shall please the Almighty to take me to himself, the event will be buried in oblivion I will not add another line, only to assure you, while life and sense remain, I will be your faithful

CAROLINE MELMOTH.

LETTER LXXI.

To WILLIAM STANHOPE, Esq;

St James's Square, February 9

In vain I every art essay,
To pluck the envenom'd shaft away,
That wrankles in my heart

IN vain I have recourse to what the world calls pleasure, but it will not do I have tried all things, but succeed in none!—I sought to lose the remembrance of one woman's perfidy in the smiles of the multitude—When I beheld a woman whose beauty was dignified by innocence, such I cried was once my Caroline; did the wanton seek to allure me, the reflection, that the abandoned Caroline was one of these, cast a veil over their smiles. —In wine I attempted to drown my passion, but the next morning I was still more wretched. O Stanhope I still love, doat to distraction on the guilty creature. How can that love subsist which was founded on esteem, now that basis is gone?

An accident, which happened a few days since, has awakened all my love, and kindled desires which once the purity of my passion forbad me to think of. Why did not I indulge them? Why not take my share in pleasures she bestows on all in common?—No, the remembrance of what I once thought her, would pall every rapture she now could give. But to the incident. I lately became acquainted with Colonel Clayton, the nephew of Lord D— in your neighbourhood, he is a sensible young fellow, and has seen a great deal of the world, as well as life. Some nights ago we supped at the Turk's-head, in Gerrard-street. The bottle passed freely, and we were all elevated.—Clayton and I walked together towards our respective homes, but were stopped by a concourse of people in an adjoining street, who had been alarmed by a fire. Humanity demanded our assistance. We made our way to the house which seemed in most danger. —A sash was thrown up, and a female appeared at the window. the people called to her to leap down, and she seemed as if going to follow their advice.—We both conjured her not to run the risk, but trust to us.—But I find it necessary to digress a little to tell you, that Clayton was very chagrin, having been disappointed of one of the most lovely girls in the world, one who had been in high life, but was now coming under the protection of your old friend Henley.

Well,

Well, we forced our way into the house, and both together rushed up stairs Clayton first ran into the room and exclaimed, "by heaven the lovely girl who was this night to have made me happy!" I was close behind him, think, Stanhope, what were my sensations, when I beheld my once loved Caroline She instantly knew me, and shrieked out, I caught her in my arms "O my beloved," cried I, "is it given thy Darnley to rescue thee?" What became of Clayton I know not, my whole soul was taken up with the charming creature, senseless in my arms I hurried out of the house with her, and conveyed her to a public house just by I placed her on a chair, and reclined her lovely face on my shoulder ——It was then, Stanhope, I feasted my eyes with beauties, which, but to think of, would fire an anchorite Her head-dress, the most becoming in the world, was disordered, her charming hair strayed on her forehead and neck! that neck, the loveliest ever gazed on by man, half exposed, the handkerchief, which she had thrown over it, being buttoned in her gown by one button —Think what a situation was mine, to have the most lovely, most beloved of women, half naked in my arms could you have withstood the temptation? I pressed her balmy lips, and snatched ten thousand kisses from her lovely breast, I did not, however, neglect the means of restoring her to sense. Heavens! what joy I expressed when she opened her eyes, and fixed them on me —Clayton's exclamation recurred to me; my former sufferings returned, and tho' I was mad with desire, I despised the object —What an angel I once thought her! O, Stanhope, how could such a woman fall? If gratitude to her benefactors,—if gratitude to the man who adored her, and still feels passions for her, no other woman can inspire; if gratitude to heaven for bestowing an angelic form, with an understanding equalled by few, and which vice alone perverted But in the words of Inatulla the Persian, I from experience can say; "When fate wrote down the fair catalogue of female virtues, a blot fell upon gratitude from his pen"

, The remainder of Sir George Darnley's letter is omitted, as Miss Melmoth in the next, gives a circumstantial account of his proceedings.

LETTER LXXII.

To Miss Vere.

March 9

AH my dearest Sidney! if I have been a murmurer at the decrees of providence surely I may stand excused Am I not marked out by adverse fortune to endure the sharpest pangs of heart rending misery? Yet what were all my former sufferings compared to this last stroke, that would nigh reduced me to death? My brain shattered,—my heart broken Had not reason left its seat I could not have survived Ah, can I thank their care, who restored me to the further knowledge of woe? Why did they not suffer me peaceably to sink into that grave, where alone rest for griefs like mine can be obtained? There and there only can I loose the remembrance of all my sufferings —Then, perhaps would my insatiable enemies be induced, from the sense that I could no longer feel sorrow, to do me that justice they now deny me Then Darnley, poor deluded Darnley! how will thy soul be racked with the torturing reflection of the injuries thou hast done me then may you exclaim how wretched you are, but then you will be ready to allow that the wretched—lost—abandoned—Caroline deserved not those cruel epithets

I had, you know, my only friend and comfort, a little recovered my former ill-fortune, and began to taste a small degree of tranquility, that is, I was grown familiar with my distresses but now alas! every remote idea of content is torn from my breast, and my only wish is to lose reflection in endless—night—I must take time—being still extremely low—to collect my fugitive reason, and endeavor to explain to you this new source of misery, which has broken its bounds, and almost overwhelmed me in dark despair—The task is at present too much for me; my tears—I cannot yet proceed,——

* * *

March 10

After I had dispatched my very long letter to you of the fifth and sixth of last month, from the events of the day, I found myself incapable of composing my thoughts, or settling to business. I made a melancholy retrospect on the last sad months of my momentous life, and filled with grief, thus naturally inspired, went to bed Falling to sleep while my spirits were thus agitated, I had the most frightful dreams, but was awaked from my shocking visions, by the repeated cries of fire! fire! I leaped out of bed, and ran in terror to the window, the sash of which I threw up, and plainly saw the spreading flames, which threatened to burst into my chamber I ran wildly backwards and forwards from the bed to the window, and mechanically put on some of my cloaths, for I am sure I knew not what I was about, as I made no attempt to get out of the door.

 door.

door. I fancy I made some attempt to get out of the window, for some people cried out to me not to leap down, for they would rescue me at the hazard of their lives. Presently two gentlemen rushed into the room, where I was half-dead with terror. —The first who entered made some exclamation, what I knew not, but good God what were my emotions, when in the other I beheld Sir George Darnley! I shrieked and sprang involuntarily toward him, he caught me in his arms.—The tenderness of his expressions—his looks—I was overpowered, and lost all sense and motion.—When I recovered from my state of happy insensibility, I found myself in a strange place, reclining on Darnley's arms, who was rubbing my temples with eau-de-luce. He perceived my returning sense,—he pressed his face to mine, and clasping me to his bosom, breathed out the most ardent thanks to heaven for restoring me to life and him. Ah! my Sidney! what sounds were these! who can describe my transports. "Is it possible!" cried I, gently attempting to disengage myself from his incircling arms, "can I be so blest as to hear you acknowledge you still love me? What a reward is this for all my sorrow! Love you!" repeated he, "by heaven I do, I ever must. Oh! Caroline," bursting from me, "had you been innocent you had been an angel.—Why were you not so?—Or why was I undeceived?—Cruel, lost, abandoned, faithless Caroline!"—

"Kill me! kill me at once," I exclaimed. "in mercy rid me of that life you vainly preserved.—O Darnley! Can you yet believe me guilty of those horrid crimes laid to my charge? Hear me, on my knees I implore you, stay and hear me. I am not, I am not guilty.—I see,—I behold the tenderness springing to your eyes.—Reflect on all my past behaviour, in what did I betray a propensity to vice? Suffer your heart my dear Darnley to plead for the

much

much injured Caroline —One day my innocence may be fully proved—then will you"——

"Your innocence! Caroline! Ah no The proofs of your infamy were too incontestible —But rise, madam Why your bended knees, uplifted hands and streaming eyes to me? Think not Caroline your artful blandishments will have any effect on me·—I know you —I love you still;—but yet despise you —I leave you to the life you choose to lead.—You are at liberty to fulfil your licentious engagement with Colonel Clayton I will send him to you he and Mrs Henley may console you, for what you have lost in me I will fly, fly far from you You Caroline have this triumph, you have made miserable the man, whose only wish, while he thought you virtuous, was to have made you the happiest of women. But I leave you this is the last time you will ever behold the most wretched of mankind"

"Stay!—I conjure you stay —You must not, shall not leave me —Darnley, the poor ill-fated, wretched Caroline calls —Stay and be witness of her death!—But I exclaimed to the winds?—he inhumanly left me, wild and frantic with despair —Madly, I would have followed, but was opposed by the wretch Clayton and others I fell into a violent hysteric fit Their too officious care recovered me, and I found my self with that vile Clayton and some strange woman, who endeavored to sooth me into calmness.

I stared wildly· "where,——where is he? Why, why have you taken him from me? He must, he shall be convinced of my innocence O Miss Grafton," lifting up my eyes and clasped hands, "now, now is your triumph complete —now may you trample on all that remains of the undone Caroline! Oh! my bursting brain.--O that I were mad indeed. Who, who are you?---Where am I? You are not Mrs Henley are you?

" No, madam," said the woman curtsying

" What do you do here? I hastily interrogated Colonel Clayton · leave me, " for heaven's sake leave me and my unheard of miseries together Do not stay to disturb my last moments too many have you helped to embitter But they soon will be over --my heart is broke,---my brain shattered,---reputation blasted---left in despair---What further injuries would you do me?"

" I wish not to do you any," answered he, " I have the highest and most tender regard for you, permit me to convince you, I am sincere in what I say ---My good woman" continued he," you may quit the room"——

" No, good woman," cried I starting up, for she was going, " do not leave the room it will be abundantly sufficient for that gentleman to leave it, or allow me to leave him"——

" No, madam," said Clayton, coming up to me and taking both my hands " I cannot, will not part with you Sir George Darnley has resigned all pretensions to you, and given you up to me I once lost an opportunity with you, but I shall now play another game."

I fixed my eyes on him, but was unable to speak, or oppose him He placed me on a chair, seating himself by me, still holding my hands he proceeded thus. " I perceive you have jilted Sir George ---I do not wonder at his resentment, I am sure he must have been generous ---But I have taken so great a fancy to you, that I am determined to supply his place ---I have sworn, never to settle on any woman; but you may depend on my honor if you are faithful to me, I will not be ungrateful Say my charming angel, shall we this moment enter into engagements I will seal my agreement on your lovely lips" at the same time attempting to kiss me and take other liberties, which

quickly

quickly rouzed me from my ſtupor.---I ſtarted from his graſp and flew towards the door, he placed himſelf between that and me. "Come, come, why this obſtinacy? theſe affected coy airs? you have deceived Sir George Darnley, but I am too knowing to be taken in. Conſent to bleſs me, by heaven you ſhall not repent it —— Why this reſiſtance? Why will you oblige me to uſe leſs gentle methods than I wiſh to do? You cannot eſcape me, why do you ſtruggle thus?"

"Have mercy, have mercy!" cried I, ſinking down on my knees "Oh! do not attempt the ruin of one whom heaven has forſaken. Suffer my tears, dear, dear Sir, ſuffer my intreaties to call forth that honor, I once found in you —Depart not from the ſacred character you then ſuſtained —O do not join with the moſt cruel of wretches, to drive to deſpair one, who if ſhe ever offended you, will ſoon be incapable of ever doing ſo again —O mercy! mercy!—O good God! ſtrike me this inſtant dead! I cannot—will not outlive theſe indignities —Help, if you are a woman, help the moſt forlorn of your ſex!"

Oh my Sidney, think what I ſuffered! The vile wretch ſtill ſtruggling with your poor Caroline, already worn down with grief —I heard a voice moſt ſeaſonably at the door "I know it is her voice —I will go in,—people, at your peril keep me from entering." The door at length was opened, and my dear good Mrs Johnſon flew to me, "O take me, take me away!" was all I could utter, I fell ſenſeleſs into her arms She ſtayed not to recover me there, but aſſiſted to carry me home to her lodgings, which were within a few doors —For eight and forty hours, ſhe tells me, I fell from one fit to another, every one of which they thought would be my laſt. Mrs Johnſon informed you what followed. Had not that ceſſation of reaſon befallen me, it would have been impossible for a human being to have sustained life But now, memory returns, and the keenest pangs intrude.

Upon a thorough retrospect, I think I can say, hope never yet quite forsook me I still tacitly flattered myself, that were it possible to meet any of those, who thought I had injured them, truth might prevail There is something the writers say in genuine truth, which will shine conspicuous through clouds of falshood. how are they—how was I deceived!

Tell me, my dearest Sidney, what have I further to do, crawling on this earth?—'Tis not my resting place Still must my wearied eye-lids vainly wake "in tedious expectation of thy peace." O all-consolating death?

* * *

March, 11

I am calm, my Sidney, but it does not appear so much to me, the unrepining resignation religion tells us, we ought to pay to the dispensations of providence, no, I will not deceive you, I cannot myself—Have you not observed, that the further people advance in life, the less they are affected with loss of friends? I am grown old in affliction Few, but evil, very evil have been the days of my pilgrimage Ancient persons receive the news of a dear friend's death with little emotion, from the certainty of their speedy meeting again. thus have I parted with the only hope which has sustained me thro' the latter part of my life. I am morally certain I soon shall meet that hope in heaven So you see there is still a kind of, to use the expression, desperate hope remaining

But still think not, I shall quit this scene, "Nor cast one longing ling'ring look behind" "On some

ſome loved breaſt the parting ſoul reſides," ſo will mine on thee; thou deareſt, beſt, moſt faithful of friends

Accept, my amiable, my ever eſteemed Sidney, accept my ſincere wiſhes for your proſperity May you never experience more infelicity, than your ſenſible heart has ſuſtained, by your generous participation of my troubles, rejoice, my love, that they ſoon will ceaſe And may you never want ſo faithful, ſo good, ſo tender a friend as I have ever found in you O, my Sidney, the heart, that has almoſt left beating for its own griefs, melts when it thinks what your's will feel at your final ſeparation. But when time has mellowed the affliction into a pleaſingly-painful remembrance, then will you truly rejoice, (as I do in proſpect) that an end was ſo early put to the unhappy life of your ever, ever faithful

CAROLINE MELMOTH

LETTER LXXIII

To Miſs MELMOTH.

Vere Park, March 14

YOUR long letter, my beloved Caroline, well nigh killed me. Great and ſevere are your trials, my amiable lovely friend,—but do not deſpair, I ſee happier days await you without that hope I could not have ſurvived the grief your diſtreſſes cauſed me

Do not affirm Sir George Darnley is blind to conviction; I truſt in heaven he will ſoon be ſenſible of your exalted merit, and then you muſt be happy—His ſufferings, my dear Caroline, muſt be exquiſite.—His love for you plainly appeared, even when

when he cruelly deserted you — Poor infatuated man!—I sincerely pity him I dare say, on reflection, you will do the same

I repeat, do not give yourself over to despair, things must soon wear another face, and a more frightful form, I think, your affairs cannot assume, than they have done, unless the devil's vice-gerent, Mrs Henley, should get you into her trammels

But you must, you shall be happy, and I hope, under heaven, your devoted faithful Sidney, may be an humble means of contributing towards the accomplishment of it

Yesterday morning Lady Betty Crauford called upon me, and seeing me very melancholy, as I have been a long time, insisted on my taking an airing with her

She pressed me to tell her the cause of my dejection, I said, I had heard some news from a very dear friend, that had put me exceedingly out of spirits, and added, "every little, joined to my domestic uneasiness, was sufficient to render me very ill company, as I doubt I am so to you now

"I do not wonder at your being dull at home, with leading the melancholy life you do but why do you not oftner come to us? We should be happy to see you—We shall have company down soon from London two beaux I assure you One of them is a very clever agreeable man, and a particular friend of all our family."

"Do I know him," I carelessly asked "I really do not know—His name is Clayton, and he is colonel in the guards."

Clayton? exclaimed I hastily, "Colonel Clayton, did your ladyship say"

"Yes, you know him I find"

"I am a stranger to his person," said I, rather more composed, "but I am not so either to his name or character, and wonder much to hear you say

say he is a particular friend of your family, since he is unworthy the notice of any less despicable than himself"

"Good God! you astonish me exceedingly Miss Vere, to hear you exclaim thus against Colonel Clayton, whom I know to be a man of strict honor, who is an ornament to his profession, and a treasure to his acquaintance"

"I beg your pardon Lady Betty, for thus freely delivering my sentiments of your friend—But myself, and one whom I love above the world, have suffered too much from Colonel Clayton, to hear him praised so unjustly as you have praised him, and be silent I hope I shall know when he is at Crauford manor, that I may avoid him as I would a pestilence"

"Indeed but you must not I feel myself strongly interested in this affair, and you must give me leave to say, my dear Miss Vere, that I insist on the Colonel's having an opportunity of clearing himself, which I am certain he can, and will do, from these unjust prejudices"

"Indeed, Lady Betty, they are not unjust, nor must you be offended"——

"I am not so my dear. but you must allow yourself to be convinced, that you have been misinformed."

"Would to heaven it may prove so.—If he is the man of honor you pronounce him, he yet may have it in his power to repair the injury he has done my lovely friend, I will then freely forgive him the irreparable one I have sustained thro' his means"

"I cannot imagine how you can have sustained injuries from a man you never saw, it appears very mysterious to me"

"I cannot at present unfold it, but you would be convinced of the reality, were I at liberty to disclose it. But when will he be with you? He may yet do do my amiable friend signal service, as he, and he only, can fully clear up an affair, which has occasioned great misery and distress to the most worthy bosom in the world."

"I dare say, nay, I can venture to affirm, Colonel Clayton never wilfully gave a moments pain to any human being, and if he has, unwillingly, to your friend, I know he will do all in his power to remedy it."

We soon after parted. Lady Betty has promised to let me know of his arrival, and added, "I do not doubt when you see the Colonel, you will allow him all the merit he deserves."

Now, my beloved Caroline, I must give way to hope, and so must you — Yes, my adorable friend, you will be happy — restored to the heart and esteem of all those you love. Colonel Clayton, if a man of honor, may unravel that vile plot of the infernal Grafton; you did not suspect him of being concerned—but then his subsequent behaviour—well, I must suspend my judgment till I see him.—If thro' his means I behold an end of my Caroline's sufferings, I shall readily pardon the ills I have, and may endure, by his procuring me a mother-in-law; I suppose you are aware that your Clayton and her's is one and the same.

Adieu my best love—Take care of your health, for the sake of your ever faithful

SIDNEY VERE.

LET-

LETTER LXXIV.

To Miſs MELMOTH.

Vere-park, March 20.

LAST night Lady Betty ſent me a note apprizing me of the arrival of Colonel Clayton, and that ſhe had in part acquainted him with her reaſons for requeſting a conference between us. This morning I went to Crauſurd manor, and was uſhered into Lady Betty's dreſſing-room.

"Does not Colonel Clayton expreſs ſome ſurprize at the ſingularity of a requeſted conference, with a young woman an entire ſtranger to him?"

"He is all impatience to ſee you, and to make what reparation he can for any failures in his Conduct, that can have given pain to you or your friend."—At theſe words a ſervant entered with Colonel Clayton's compliments, and begged we would allow him to wait on us, Lady Betty anſwered, we would be happy to ſee him.

Tho' I had endeavoured to arm myſelf with reſolution, yet I felt ſtrangely fluttered at his appearance.—He bowed very reſpectfully.—"I hope, ladies," ſays he, "you will not blame me for intruding on your company, but the diſtreſs I feel, while I am ſenſible I labor under the imputation of injuring this lady, will plead my excuſe. In what, madam," addreſſing me with a penſive air, "have I been ſo unfortunate as to incur your diſpleaſure. I never willingly cauſed pain to any one, nor can I think it poſſible I could have offended a lady, whom till this moment I never beheld; and ſo far from feeling any diſpoſition to injure, I ſhould be ready to teſtify, at the hazard of my life, the reſpect her preſence has inſpired me with."

By

By this time I assumed a little more courage— "As to what more materially regards my affairs, Sir, is not of the least consequence, compared to the sufferings of a most amiable and virtuous young lady."

Sufferings! madam, and I the author of them, you astonish me prodigiously."

I beg your pardon, Sir,—nay, you must grant it me, "if the uncommon friendship I feel for this young lady, should induce me to speak with too great warmth and little respect."

"I find in myself, madam, so sincere an inclination to be thought better of by you, that I will readily excuse any thing but being kept longer in suspence."

"To be short, do you remember, Sir, an incident which happened the beginning of last September, you, and another gentleman of the army whose name is Campbell, met two ladies, and attended them to the museum gardens*."

"I very well remember the adventure you speak of." "And pray, Sir, what did you think of those ladies? I thought of them, madam, as I had been informed by Captain Campbell they were, two ladies of pleasure. The lady who fell to my share, was exquisitely beautiful."

"Did you think her such as you named, Sir?"

"Her freely entering the house, whither her companion and mine had gone before, gave me sufficient reason to imagine I should not injure her by such a supposition—

"But her behaviour when there, Sir"——

——"Did not at all correspond with my thoughts of her I own: For when, as I supposed myself authorized, I began to treat her with some degree of freedom, she repulsed me with such be-

"coming

* See Letter, 54.

coming dignity as awed me, but convinced she would never have come thither, if she had any regard for her reputation, I attempted still greater liberties but never shall I forget the nobleness of her sentiments, or the manner in which she laid claim to my protection I have, I own madam, indulged myself in some liberties with the fair-sex, but I have too great reverence for virtue, to attempt to destroy it · never will any woman at the last day lift up her hands against me as her destroyer, 'tis true, that when going down the slippery path of vice, I have not been very ready to help them up again: but to return to the lady—Convinced she was a woman of virtue, I behaved honorably to her, as indeed I could do no other, the respect and compassion she inspired me with, demanded it. I procured a chair for her—As she was coming out of the house, I believe she saw somebody she knew pass by in a chariot, for she turned pale as ashes, and drew back"

"From that fatal adventure may my dear, my valued friend, date all her miseries. There is no doubt, but had this diabolical scheme failed, there were others equally destructive to her reputation and peace.—But how could you, Colonel Clayton, join with those infernal wretches in this concerted plot?

"For heaven's sake, my dear Miss Vere, harbor not so vile a thought of me.—I would protect innocence to the last drop of my blood, and would not join in an infamous plot to gain an empire. The morning of that day Campbel called on me, and after some trifling chat, asked me in a careless way, if I was disposed for a frolic that afternoon I at first refused, as I knew his frolics in general suited not my taste. O you must go, said he, it is to meet two fine girls who have a mind to pass an hour or two at our friend Henley's. Errington, continued

nued he, was to have been one of their squires, but he is engaged, and I must not diappoint them so if you will go, I will call for you I hope, madam, you will do me the justice to believe I had not any knowledge of base designs. I cautioned the lady against trusting her false friend, as, without arrogating much merit to myself, she might have met with men who would have taken dishonourable advantages of such an opportunity"

"I called at Campbel's lodging, and at the guard, but could not find him I was then obliged to leave town for a few days, and on my return, found he had obtained absence of leave for three *months, which confirmed me in the opinion* that he could not justify himself in this strange affair"

I thought it necessary to let Colonel Clayton into the particulars of your momentous life, both he and lady Betty were greatly affected by the mournful recital. He swore he would never rest till he had, as far as was in his power, cleared your innocence, and made you happy

He continued: "The moment I saw Miss Melmoth with Mrs Henley, I own I changed my sentiments greatly in her disfavor. I own too I was happy in the knowledge of so lovely a girl being within my reach When I found her not with the old woman at night, as I had expected, I left the house, there b ing no temptation strong enough to keep me, and in going home I met Sir George Darnley Our acquaintance had not been long, but intimate for the time. I told him of my recent disappointment in the finest creature I had ever seen He said you must toast her then to night at the tavern, and since she will not bless your arms, she must crown your bumpers"

"I did not enter into particulars, as Sir George *seemed to express no curiosity concerning her* —We happened to fall in with some of our mutual friends,

friends, and went to the Turk's Head, in Gerrard Street. The bottle was pushed about briskly, Sir George being the greatest promoter, a circumstance I never before observed in him. In consequence of toasting freely, my spirits were greatly exhilarated; thus, under the unhappy influence of wine, and the mistaken notion of Miss Melmoth's being the faithless mistress of Sir George Darnley, gave occasion of a behaviour I shall ever regret."

"I must intreat you, madam, to interceed with your charming friend in my behalf, yet not till I have done something to deserve it. I would write to Sir George, did I with any certainty know his address; but as soon as I get to town, [and you will permit me, my dear lady Betty, to shorten my visit on this occasion] I will fly to him, and ease the hearts of two deserving people."

"And now," said lady Betty, "may I congratulate you, Colonel, for having dissipated the cloud which enveloped your honor in Miss Vere's eyes."

"I fear not," said he, rising and taking my hand. "Tell me, my charming judge, am I deceived when I say I am apprehensive there is still a doubt subsisting in your bosom? you cannot yet acquit the prisoner at the bar."

"That you have acted the part of a man of honor, in the case of my beloved friend, I will allow; but I doubt, Colonel, there is another bill of indictment filed against you, which will prove that innocence has not always been protected by you."

"Another bill, my dear Miss Vere! you will permit me, I hope, to plead not guilty?"

"What without being heard Colonel?"

"Only the privilege of the bar Lady Betty."

"Indeed, Sir, I shall be very happy to find you innocent of this heavy charge but you have taken such a weight of sorrow off my heart in the flatter-

ing

ing hope of my dear Caroline's innocence being fully proved, that I am inclined to pardon every other offence the culprit may have committed, and will, if you please, dismiss the court."

"When a prosecution has commenced and not carried on, madam, the delinquent has a right to lay an indictment for defamation not that I shall do so, but I must intreat you to let me hear now all that can be alledged against me I am sanguine perhaps, in saying I am morally certain I shall be discharged the court with honor. Come my gentle arbitress, question me as you please, and be assured that not even the apprehension of losing your esteem for ever, shall in the smallest point tempt me to deviate from the strictest truth."

I bowed to his compliment, and asked him, "if when he was quartered at—in Gloucestershire, he was not acquainted with a family named Arnold?"

"Aye, very well, to my cost with one of the family, madam, the eldest daughter, but I hope you do not"——

"I wish I did not, Sir But say can you still affirm you never injured innocence?"

"Yes, madam, truly, as I would answer at my last trial I much fear Miss Arnold had never much innocence to boast of, if she had even worn the appearance of it, I should have reverenced that appearance I suppose, madam, by your question, you are not ignorant of my connection with Miss Arnold, she had the same tho' secretly with two officers in the same regiment, one of whom got an exchange that he might be rid of her—She had the good fortune to meet with men who did not make a practice of boasting of their amours, so that her reputation was not intirely lost when I met with her I liked her very much, the more so, as she was in a manner thrown in my way my advances were very acceptable to her, and upon my being

being ordered to march to Coventry, she pleaded so effectually with me, that I took her with me. We lived there in great harmony. In the winter I took her to town, where soon I discovered her in an affair with my servant, him I instantly discharged, and was determined to have no further connection with her, but to make some provision for her at a distance I did not deliberate long, for in two days my lady decamped, having first broke open a bureau, out of which she took in money and bills about two hundred pounds, and a very fine diamond ring ---In the heat of my resentment I obtained a warrant to apprehend both her and my servant, but hearing he was gone off to France and left her in distress, I left them to their fate"

"Good God!" I exclaimed, "what wretches are there in the world ---" You say, Sir, you have indulged yourself in some liberties with our sex, see what inconveniences attend such indulgences Here is the state of the case as related by Miss Arnold, whom I am so unhappy as to have for a mother-in-law Her story wrought so on my heart, that I introduced her into my family, and by her art she has made herself the mistress of it"

I gave Colonel Clayton the manuscript ---" I am not to learn," said he, "the consummate art of that infamous creature, but I am excessively concerned to hear you are so intimately connected with her" After he had read her fine history, he made many judicious remarks, with great sense and truth. In short, notwithstanding the many unhappy hours he has unknowingly occasioned, if he should succeed ---as I have not the least doubt he will in your cause, what reward shall we bestow? Do you think the heart of your little Sidney will be worth his acceptance; For I feel I shall be half in love with him,

him Have I not sent you a rich cordial ?----You must now soon be well, and that you may be soon happy is the unceasing prayer of

Your

SIDNEY VERE

LETTER LXXV.

To Miss VERE.

March 29

INfinite are my obligations to you my dear, my only friend—but never, never can I profit by them No, my Sidney ——vain are your wishes, your prayers, your Caroline was not born to experience any other than the ills of life.—Oh that it were over !

Sir George must by this time have heard Colonel Clayton's relation, but he is deaf—inexorable or perhaps he had engaged too far with my cruel prosecutor.—Ah ! may he then never know my innocence, and yet must she have such a triumph—my God ! his wife —I cannot bear that thought —Sidney ! he will marry her—Marry my greatest enemy —Oh God ! I saw the coach yesterday her arms quartered with his —It is too much —Is it of consequence I must bear these ills ?—What wise purposes can it answer ? Mrs Johnson enquired at the coach-maker's, he said he was working with the utmost haste, as the wedding only waited for him —What anguish did the account give me——And will he become her husband ?—Is it thus Sidney

Sidney my injuries are to be repaired ——Thus I am to be made happy ?—Vain, vain hope!—Ah my Sidney weary not heaven with petitions for an unhappy victim of its divine wrath, but let your only prayer be that I may be released by a speedy death—I cannot write—My thoughts are all distraction it is with difficulty I hold my pen to tell you how dear you are to the wretched

CAROLINE MELMOTH.

LETTER LXXVI.

To Miss VERE.

April 4

HEAVEN has at last, my dearest Sidney, raised me up a friend, who is determined to stand forth the champion of my innocence If Colonel Clayton undertakes my cause, I hope it will not prove an arduous one—But what then will become of Sir George Darnley? He will then be convinced of the injustice of my sufferings—and be miserable, unless the diabolical arts of his lady still keep him in ignorance You will wonder to hear me thus calmly speak of that so-much-dreaded event; O Sidney it has cost me many pangs—but the fatal struggle is over, and I think the cruel treatment I received when last I beheld him, has in some measure awakened—or rather given birth to a sentiment I was ever a stranger to,—I feel a kind of resentment towards him.—Yet he thought me the wretch he he called me.—Ah! my imagination paints him to me all penitence and tenderneſs—Avaunt thou deceitful phantom—I muſt not think of thee—Thou art now another's right ——

But I was going to tell you of an adventure: I will endeavour to proceed with regularity

Mrs. Johnſon has prevailed on me to take airing, which I do every day, generally I take a coach to Hyde-park, and walk for ſome time there Yeſterday morning finding myſelf fatigued, I reſted myſelf againſt a rail I had not been long in this ſituation abſorbed in thought, ere I was rouzed from my reſverie by ſome gentlemen galloping by, I looked up and immediately recognized one in the perſon of Sir John Evelin he knew me inſtantly and haſtily jumped from his horſe —" Heaven has heard my prayer, ſaid he, and I have found you I felt very much diſordered, and could not at that moment command words He gazed earneſtly in my face —" Ah! my adorable Miſs Melmoth, what have I endured ſince laſt I parted from you! little did I then think to ſee you thus"—His voice faltered---he pauſed.——

" To ſee me," ſaid I, " an outcaſt, driven from ſociety, branded with infamy, and only conſcious innocence my ſupport"---Tears forced a paſſage, ---I could not proceed

" Yes you muſt-- I am convinced you are innocent But this, my dear madam, is no place to hold a conference in, will you permit me to attend you home, it may be in my power to diſpel the clouds that have enveloped you, if not, my protection you may claim, ſince in ſpite of every effort you ſtill hold the ſame place in my eſteem you ever did And were all the world againſt you, I would at the hazard of my life protect and defend you from that world inſenſible of your merit You once ſaid," continued he, with tenderneſs in his eyes,

eyes, "you considered me as a friend, may I hope you still look on me in that light, my study shall be to deserve that distinction"

"Seldom does the creature abandoned to misfortune meet with such generosity I have received proofs already, Sir, of your goodness, ah! do not then condemn me for readily giving you belief. I was never of a suspicious temper 'till fatal experience taught me how dangerous it was to rely on those, whom interest, or any sinister view might bias but I ever discovered such true nobleness of mind in you, that gave birth to, and encreased my esteem for you I must,—I will confide in you"

We soon reached that end next Piccadilly, and there took a coach and proceeded to my lodgings. In our way thither, I related to him in a summary way my story, he was greatly affected at it He told me, he believed what I had recited that he had ever thought me innocent, and that Miss Gratton's principles were no strangers to him He made no doubt but in a short time the whole affair would be cleared up, and intreated I would look on him as one born only for my service, and command whatever was his accordingly He desired permission to wait on me the next day, which his impatience prompted him to do early in the morning, when he acquainted me Lord L was in France; but that neither difficulty or danger should deter him from obliging Lord L to clear my fame. After a long conversation he obliquely hinted his former passion I chose not to understand him, but at the same time let him see how sensible I was of his merit and generosity In the most delicate manner he pressed me to receive some pecuniary assistance, which however I absolutely refused —

He begs me to allow him to visit me sometimes. —I saw every moment he was ready to declare his real motives O[illegible] I were restored to the bosom

 of

of my benefactress, and that the worthy Evelin would be content with my friendship—my esteem; then would my heart feel rest, happy I can never be.

I could regard and love him as a brother, my heart is now incapable of any other sentiment.—Darnley exhausted all my stock of tenderness—Yet tell me, my dear Sidney, what must I do with this worthy amiable man? give me your advice—Ought not his respectful silence to have weight with me. He has intitled himself to my highest esteem, this he possessed even when my attachment to Sir George was strongest. Tell me what you would do in my situation, and I will conform to your dictates be they what they will—

Adieu, ever Your's,

CAROLINE MELMOTH.

LETTER LXXVII.

To Miss MELMOTH.

Vere-Park, April 7.

I Am perplexed and confounded at Clayton's silence—Lady Betty insists he will do all he can—yet should he fail—I know not what to think.

Amiable worthy Evelin! What a soul has that man! you pay, my beloved Caroline, great deference to your Sidney, ah, does not your own heart suggest what you ought to do—But you are afraid to follow its dictates I fear Sir George is not worthy of you, how eminently has the amiable Evelin ever shewn his disinterested love for you A fatal prepossession has prevented your doing justice to his merit——

I:

In your situation it would be madness—absolute phrenzy to refuse him—Consider the advantages arising from such an union, many people, who will look askance at Caroline Melmoth, will be happy to be received and distinguished by Lady Evelin. This then, is my advice, and as I would do in your case you own a great esteem for him, is not that the surest base to build love on?—undoubtedly —The obligations you are under to him—His amiable disposition considered—his immense fortune, least thought of by you—his unprecedented passion, ever constant, ever hopeless all this surely lays claim to your gratitude, and how can you shew it in a more lively manner, than by devoting your life to him, and by that constituting his felicity?

You have tasted the fountain of love, and found it bitter of flavor, and filled with thorns——

Sir John Evelin is a man who bears a universal good character—One who must render a sensible mind happy—Does not such a man deserve some sacrifice to be made him? Darnley is perhaps by this time married, you must think, nay you will not I am sure think of him more—You cannot determine to live for ever single, an old maid!—A character ever ridiculed—If you refuse him, believe me, you will repent it.—Such offers are not to be expected often.

It will be long my sweet girl ere I shall have it in my power to receive you. I want a year and half of coming of age, or I would bear you to some peaceful retreat. Yet think not "thou wert born to blush unseen, and lose thy sweetness on the desart air" No I can never believe you were, but to live blest and blessing.

You can never love a second time with the fervency you have already experienced? if, then you hereafter marry, most likely it will be some one still less esteemed by you than Sir John. Endeavor

to behold h m with a partial eye; and tell me, i
your next, you loſe the repugnance you a preſe
feel, when you think of rewarding him in th
only manner he can be rewarded Adieu,

SIDNEY VIP

LETTER LXXVIII

To Miſs VERE.

April 11

WHAT ſhall I do with this amiable man—th Sir John Evelin? He is ever con er ing be nefits, yet in ſuch manner as gives me pleaſu while it oppreſſes me, not having it in my powe to return them This morning Miſs Maria Ch mers (the young woman at Stevens's, to whom I owed that kind caution) came to me, and thank me for the generous proviſion made for her of fif pounds a year for life, the bond was ſent her la night as from me You may believe I was ſurpriz but I can ſcarce ſay whether that ſentiment o ad miration of Sir John's worth was greateſt Ho delicate, how engaging ſuch behavior! Mrs Jo ſon has a ſettlement of a hundred a year in th ſame genteel manner—How do theſe actions e hance my former obligations towards him—M eſteem, my gratitude increaſe every day, my I could almoſt ſay without bounds

He was with me laſt night, but gave not ne le hint of his intentions, which certainly renders th favor greater

His lips are ſilent, yet I can ſee the ſtruggle h has to reſtrain a paſſion viſible in his every look How kind, how truly noble!—Intitled as he is t my grateful eſteem, he yet receives the ſmall

mar

marks of it, as the highest honor confered on him. It pains me very much sometimes, because I cannot act as you tell me I ought: but yet should the tender affection of such a man be repaid with, at best, a divided heart?—Should he not alone fill the breast of the most amiable of women? But as you say, does not such a man merit some sacrifice?—Is any pain an individual can suffer too great when a general good is considered?—With an Evelin it is not in nature to be miserable.—I was unhappy in my first attachment.—It is plain Sir George Darnley was never designed for me. If he had any faults, I was blind to them, tho' perhaps my eyes might have been opened when too late: but I behold Sir John Evelin without the mist of passion, and find, worth, discretion, virtue, generosity, and nobleness of sentiment blended in his character. What estimable qualities these in a man one would wish to spend one's life with, and how seldom do we meet with them?

I repeat over the catalogue of his virtues—my reason allows them, but the heart is silent, or at least feels not that sensibility it ought. I meet him with pleasure, but his absence fills me not with inquietude.

I behold him without emotion—hear his name and voice without trembling: but then to obviate these, I conclude that the obstacles, the difficulties which attended my seeing and conversing with Sir George Darnley might, in a great measure, occasion such emotions. My senses were ever in a tumult, here all calm and serene; is it not that now happiness is in my reach, and then I was ever apprehensive of having it snatched from me?

Upon a candid examination I think, really, I love Sir John Evelin, as much as a heart, torn as mine has been, can do. And if I do not experience in his society that rapture of joy, I shall likewise miss those depths of sorrow, into which my unhappy partiality plunged me

I call reason—religion, all to my aid, but it is not in nature Sidney to divest oneself of all remembrance I wish I could but " Oh! I cannot but remember such things were, and were most dear to me " The lover will too often present himself to the imagination long after the love ought to have ceased I think of Sir George from habit, so long was he the subject of my thoughts he insensibly became a part of myself His image is ever before my eyes, I see him as he once appeared, tender, lovely, and worthy of being beloved,—but that time is now over —Colonel Clayton could not succeed.

I certainly betray a want of resolution in thus regreting an ingrate —Ah! my Sidney, could I have treated him as I have been treated by him? Offended meekness has a keen memory, I will strive to erase him from mine, at least I will prescribe rules to my pen, nor will I, if possible, mention him again, but as one who is dead, and whose death alone could have cancelled all failings

Sir John Evelin is come How shall I thank him as my heart longs to thank him, without raising hopes I cannot encourage You won't forgive me, Sidney, I must therefore quit my pen, lest I incur your further displeasure. Adieu for the present—

* * *

How politely did Sir John evade my acknowledgements, he would not suffer me to thank him; I told him, he might prevent my words but not could deter my heart from feeling the full sense of what I owed him, that heaven only, whose vicegerent I considered him, could repay him He was going to make a reply, his voice faltered—his lips trembled,

trembled, and his face was ſpread with bluſhes.—He yet was ſilent.—How did that dumb eloquence move my heart it ſuggeſted to me, my dear, what I ought to have done, but I could not follow the advice it gave me.—Tears ſtarted into my eyes.—I turned aſide to conceal my emotions.—O, why have I not a heart to beſtow!

Mrs. Johnſon coming into the room at the ſame time relieved us both from an equally-painful ſituation, tho' I believe our feelings were different. On the good woman's pouring forth her thanks, he ſtopped her, ſaying, "my worthy Mrs Johnſon conſider this trifle only as part of the debt I owe you for your care of the moſt amiable of women; were I to have given way to my gratitude, half my eſtate would have been nothing"

"God reward your goodneſs, Sir, in the next world, and if there is a poſſibility of your meeting it in this, here only" ſaid ſhe, taking and kiſſing my hand, "can you find it" I felt my color change, my whole frame was diſordered —Sir John's face was like crimſon —He took my other hand and gently preſſed it to his trembling lips —I know you will chide me, it was involuntary —I could not help throwing could water on his riſing hopes ——I curtſeyed and begged his permiſſion to retire for a few moments He ſighed deeply and bowed —I hurried from him —Mrs Johnſon followed me, ſhe found me bathed in tears —She apologized for her abruption, but ſaid ſhe could not have helped it for the world —"And ſhe muſt take the liberty to ſay, ſhe thought I was cruel to myſelf in not giving encouragement to a man formed to make me happy"

I ſpent ſome minutes before I could aſſume reſolution to go in again ——

Sir John even fearful of giving me pain, gave a turn to the converſation which had ſo much oppreſſed me, tho' it was viſibly conſtrained on both

 ſides.

fides After fpending fome time in chatting o' things equally indifferent and uninterefting he took his leave

Ah! how fincere his attachment to me! yet what modeft diffidence ----But may I not acquit my felf, my deareft Sidney of cruelty at leaft? Were the obligations of his fide, I might have made my felf an offering to him; but as it is, would it not be taking advantage of his paffion? advife me —counfel me. I will, as I have ever done, pay all due deference to the judgment of my kind, my ever dear Sidney.

Adieu, unalterably yours,

CAROLINE MELMOTH.

LETTER LXXIX

To Mifs MELMOTH.

Vere-Park, April 1[illegible]

YOU will as you ever have done, pay all due deference to my judgment—that I deny it you had you would by this time have been Lady Evelyn, a confirmation that " ftrong as proofs of holy writ"—for you are ftill Caroline Melmoth

I will make allowances for your great delicacy, but beware my dear, I have heard of fuch a foible as falfe-delicacy Now whether your laft remark in the letter before me, favors at all of this fame fpurious quality which has over-run almoft all the women of this age, or not, ftill remains a doubt with me Oppofe the delicate behavior of Sir John Evelin to your ladyfhip's, and after a fair tri-

al,

al, tell me truly which is the pureſt and moſt genuine delicacy: well, you have made the retroſpect—What is the reſult?—You are ſilent—A bluſhing down-caſt-eye denoting you are deceived in your notions of true-delicacy. You own there is more of that amiable ſentiment in Sir John Evelin's not preſſing you to confer an everlaſting happineſs on him, becauſe he appears, from circumſtances, to have a right to all you can beſtow, than in your throwing cold water on his riſing hopes, becauſe it might look as if you took advantage of his paſſion; well, I congratulate you, my dear, on your finding at length a proper notion of perſons and things.

You cannot, after this candid confeſſion, act contrary to your better judgment: before you only deceived yourſelf in your erroneous opinion of delicacy, but now you would be guilty of a crime worſe than the ſin of witchcraft. How can you evince your ſenſibility of a generous action conferred on you, unleſs you do what is in your power to repay it? You know what is in your power, and the part you ought to act. There is but one woman, and one way to reward ſuch a man. and ſhall you, out of an idle punctilio, make ſuch a man unhappy? forbid it gratitude!

Be not all angel my Caroline, let the woman a a little prevail.—Think what a triumph over your enemies, not that, that would give you pleaſure, no, I know your tender, gentle, forgiving diſpoſition too well.—But yet one would forgive a little exultation too on ſuch an occaſion, over thoſe friends who have ſo nearly completed your ruin, as near as devils themſelves could injure angels. For theſe wretches to behold the depreſſed Caroline Melmoth raiſed to ſuch an envied height; and I ſincerely hope to feel yourſelf happy,—then would you look back on the thorny path you have trod, without regret, and forward to the moſt permanent felicity.

I own I am rather surprized at not hearing from Colonel Clayton: I am apprehensive from his silence—knowing how sanguine I was, he is unwilling to disappoint me. Lady Betty too rather confirms my suspicions.

She has prevailed on my father to permit me to go to D—— races. We set off to-morrow, and shall be absent about ten days. I desire you will continue to write as usual to Vere-Park, as it is impossible to tell you our route; we propose seeing every thing curious in our way.

Let your next contain every thing as I wish, and what you can communicate with pleasure. If you do not act with your known prudence and generosity, I shall condemn, but yet forgive you.

The manner of doing trifles, gives the air of importance. Never let any one wait for a benefit you design them. Emulate the noble gracefulness of Sir John. Your heart is a very good heart, and suggests good things, put these good suggestions in execution, and be as happy as I wish you.

Adieu,

SIDNEY VERE.

LETTER LXXX.

To Miss VERE.

April ..

YOU have, I find by your letter, a clearer [illegible] of delicacy than I. — Your arguments shall have weight with me. I think of Sir George [illegible] his anxiety; it will soon become a crime to think of him.

him at all, but with indifference I mean. Sir John encreases daily in my favor. So attentive.—so delicate, yet love so apparent.—Such unexampled goodness He begged me this morning to think of something wherein he might oblige me;——Why would I not command him.——"Ah! Sir John," said I, "how am I to repay the obligations I have already received? teach me a way to shew my gratitude equal to your worth" He looked down and was silent, then raising his eyes to mine, and taking my hand, which he gently pressed, and bending his knee "Oh Miss Melmoth would you permit me to hope"—then paused "What would Sir John —what would my best friend say?"———

—"Would you, most adorable of women, accept the services of my whole life, then should that life be ever devoted to you to repay in a small degree the inestimable blessing"

"Rise Sir John," the tears starting in my eyes, "I intreat you rise And can you, best of men, wish to possess a heart unworthy of you, because an exhausted one?—Must the unparalleled affection you have shewn me be repaid by one who has wasted her whole stock of love on an ingrate? one who is poor in every sense?"

"It is your esteem—your friendship, my lovely Caroline, I wish to possess"

"These, Sir John, you have ever possessed"

"Will they then be lessened when I have a more powerful claim to them? Suffer me to receive the honor of your hand, and I will leave to time to grant the rest. My assiduity, my tenderness and love may induce you to behold me with different eyes I would chearfully forego my own happiness to facilitate yours, were there any possibility of your meeting it where you once sought it ——But that thought must not be indulged, Sir George Darnley is married, or very near it surely he has merited

merited the pain he will feel, for his blind credulity, in not suffering himself to be convinced

"There wants not these arguments to render your perfections Sir John more conspicuous I have ever had a grateful heart; nor can it be less so, but augmented by my duty And if I cannot quite divest myself of a fatal prepossession, yet an affectionate, true and faithful"—wife I would have said, but tears and sobs choaked my utterance He kissed my hand with rapture.—He was all joy

We talked of his mother He said she was the most amiable of women, and would be happy in hearing her son's approaching felicity —She had ever been acquainted with his partiality for me I told him, that the reflection of his marrying one whose character in life was doubtful, would be an allay to my happiness To satisfy me, he said, he would go to Lord L he questioned not but he should prevail on him to clear my fame.——Lord L to a man was a man of honor, tho' when a woman was concerned, would act the part of a villain. I told him I feared Lord L was an enterprizing man, and would vindicate himself but one way; that if he (Sir John) should be drawn into any dilemma in this affair, I should look upon myself as the sole occasion of it He assured me life was now become very dear to him, since I owned I had interest in it, and he should carefully preserve it for my sake, and endeavor to make me pleased with my lot—

He said he should make immediate preparations to go to Lord L—And would set out the next day—I will finish my letter when he is gone ———

* * *

April 19

I have just parted with the most amiable of men. My tears are a tribute due to his uncommon merit

When

When he took leave of me, he knelt down and repeated the moſt fervent vows of everlaſting love—I thought it was a call upon me, and in the ſame ſolemn manner I vowed to be his alone——Yet I know not how, I felt a kind of repugnance—no, it was not a repugnance neither,—I cannot find a name for it—I think of him with pleaſure in every other relation than that in which I muſt now conſider him, when I behold him in that point of view, I feel as I could not before deſcribe

Is it not owing to ſome latent remains of my former attachment? I am ſure it is not for want of endeavors that I have not rooted out that inclination, but it will not be—However, I hope I ſhall not make a worſe wife to Sir John for that—How is it I cannot forbear ſhuddering when I think of being his wife?

I wiſh he had not gone, I feel as if I was afraid he ſhould loſe ground in his abſence—Ungrateful Caroline! is it not for thee he is abſent?

O Sidney! my heart is not as it uſed to be, I am unlike myſelf in every thing but my attachment to you and when I ceaſe to love you, may the exiſtence ceaſe of your

CAROLINE MELMOTH.

LETTER LXXXI.

To Miſs VERE.

Arlington Street, April 10.

WILL my amiable Miſs Vere pardon me for being near three weeks in town, without acquainting her that I flew to execute her commiſſion,

miſſion, and to repair the injury I unwillingly offered her lovely friend.

Believe me, madam, had I met with no obſtacle, you ſhould long ſince have received the agreeable news; but on my arrival in London, I found a meſſenger from my uncle Lord D—, to whom I owe great love, and whoſe life being in imminent danger, demanded my immediate preſence in Northamptonſhire. Tho' urgent my call to my honored relation, I, yet, firſt thought of your commands.—I ran haſtily to St. James's Square, but to my unutterable concern, learnt Sir George was gone a little tour.—They could not inform me where he bent his courſe, or when he would return.

Greatly chagrined I threw myſelf into a poſt chaiſe, and with all expedition went to my uncle's. I returned from thence, after paying my laſt duties to my almoſt parent, and directly diſpatched a meſſenger to Sir George Darnley, earneſtly requeſting him to meet me at ſix in the evening, at the tavern we laſt ſupped in; as I had ſomething which nearly concerned his future peace, to communicate to him.

My next buſineſs was to go to the guard to enquire for Campbell, whom by ſome accident—or probably deſign on his ſide, I had never ſeen ſince the beginning of September. I was fortunate enough to meet him. I requeſted him to go with me to the Turk's Head, at five or ſix o'clock the evening. Having an affair of honor on my hands, in which he ſhould be umpire. I practiſed that piece of deceit to induce him, who loved to be thought of conſequence, to give Sir George a meeting; judging his evidence, which I was determined ſhould be a true one, might be of ſingular advantage to our cauſe.

At half an hour after five, Campbell and I took

our

our ſtations I had previouſly given directions that Sir George ſhould be conducted into another room, and to have word brought me the gentleman was come

Juſt as the clock ſtruck ſix I receiv'd the ſummons I went to Sir George Darnley, and told Campbell I ſhould ſoon ſend for him — He was greatly altered—a ſettled melancholy in his look, mixed with a faint curioſity

" I am come in compliance with your requeſt, Clayton, What are your commands? What can you know of conſequence to my future peace? I put off an engagement that I might obey your ſummons, tho' I cannot divine what it may prove "

" I hope, Sir George, the ſource of your felicity and laſting happineſs "

Happineſs to me! Ah, Clayton, never, " happineſs and I have long ſhaken hands, and bid an eternal adieu "——

" But ſhe is not paſt recalling, Darnley —Suppoſe I was to point her out to your view, it would be but ſome compenſation for my innocently cauſing your miſery, and the beſt of women's too "

" You talk in riddles, Colonel — I do not accuſe you of making me wretched "

" No, but I was in ſome meaſure inſtrumental to it "

" For heaven ſake, Clayton, explain yourſelf "

" My dear Darnley, do you remember the laſt time we parted from hence "

" Clayton! do not recal to my imagination thoſe curſed ſcenes —Remember! can I forget them! Is it thus you would recompenſe the injuries you talk of?—Why cannot I tear her falſe—falſe image from my heart?"

" Do not attempt it, Darnley What would your generous boſom feel on finding that much-injured-excellence, as ſhe is, innocent?"

" Innocent!

"Innocent!—Yes, Clayton, you have proved her innocence, she has deceived you as well as me."———

"By heaven! she is innocent—virtuous—I will prove it—you must, you shall be convinced."

"Clayton, tell me this glass is one solid diamond, this table beaten gold, and then tell me Caroline Melmoth is innocent—and virtuous. If this is all you have to say, farewel—Your embassy has failed, but you know her obligations are the same to you—While you are connected with her, we must be strangers—When we happen to meet again you may wish me joy, next week I am to be married to Miss Grafton."

"O Darnley,—you will then be the most wretched of men. Marry Miss Grafton! sooner marry your grave than that vile"———

—'Sir, it is not my calling you friend, shall prevent my calling such behavior insolent, and treating it as it deserves."

"Darnley, you must not leave me in anger—I never yet asserted any thing I could not prove—But why this obstinate determination, not to have your eyes opened? By heaven you shall not stir till you are convinced."——

—"Of what would you convince me, O Clayton! do not trifle with me, nor seek again to deceive me to ruin."

"I would convince you, Darnley, I am your friend—I would prove to you how much you have been deceived by the worst of women—I would demonstrate to you how cruelly unjust your censures have been on the ill-treated and amiable Miss Melmoth. I would shew you the malice of her implacable enemies who sought to destroy that virtue they could not emulate; and when they found the basis too firm to be shaken, blasted,—Curses blast them---her reputation.---Say, my dear

Sir

Sir George, could I prove this would it not be worth the staying for---and deserving the epithet I bestowed on Miss Grafton?"

"Had I listened only to the report of others, Clayton, I might have been misinformed—But these eyes were witness of her perfidy—Her letters, Oh too well I know the hand?

"My most intimate friend heard her spoken of infamously in several taverns by the most libertine of the town I too saw her, tho' then I discredited the evidence of my senses, I saw her at a genteel brothel with her cursed seducer—Do not call me obstinately bent against opening my eyes, it was long before I could be convinced of her faithlessness, the proofs were at length incontestible"

"You know, Darnley, I am afraid of no man, therefore do not suspect me capable of advancing what I cannot maintain—maintain with my life, if need require—Miss Melmoth was at the house you mention—You---I find it was, tho' that I did not know---drove by in a chariot she saw you: did you see the face of the man with her?"

"No, I did not, his face was towards the door, but from his size and Lord L's dress being described to me, I knew him"——

"You are basely informed, Sir George. I was the man with Miss Melmoth but there is one in this house that can clear up these mysterious points to you, tho' to me they are fully unravelled"——

I rang the bell, Campbell appeared—I shut the door and locked it—"Now, Campbell," said I, "if you expect to leave this room alive, declare instantly all you know of the concerted plot which ruined the reputation of Miss Melmoth The affair is well known to me, therefore deviate not from the strictest truth This gentleman is Sir George Darnley, you know him by name. By the eternal God

God that made me, I swear this pistol shall rid the world of a monster, unless you make a full confession" The rascal trembled with apprehensions I should have made my words good Sir George was all agony --- "Speak, wretch, this instant!" exclaimed he, "or I will prevent Clayton's execution"——

"My honor alone, Sir George, is concerned if he does not corroborate what I have said, it is I who will take revenge"

"Come, Campbell, for once in your life act the part of an honest man You know it is in my power to advance you by speaking to the Duke —You likewise see your life is now in my hands— One or the other by heaven shall be your portion"

Thus threatened and assured, he ventured to speak and unfolded a tale of much wonder— Poor Sir George!—What pen can describe his agony —Every faculty seemed suspended, or rather lost in attention —I never shall forget his countenance, possessed now by surprise, now by indignation, now by grief —As soon as Campbell had made his relation, I bid him leave the room, which command he hastily complied with, glad enough to escape so

Darnley remained almost motionless, leaning his head on his hands —His voice was almost smothered with sighs and sobs —I strove to sooth him, and bid him now hope for happier days —"Oh never, never, Clayton!—Oh I could have better born the confirmation of thy guilt —But to know—to find thee innocent!—Clayton, why did you undeceive me?—Why shew me the joys of heaven to snatch it from my sight for ever?—O Caroline! Caroline! thou angel-goodness —But no, thou canst not forgive —Can I ask it? I dare kneel—dare sue —Clayton, she did the same, --the lovely injured beauteous maid knelt to me---and Oh! distraction

seize

seize me-- knelt---implored in vain"

I pleaded a long time the matchless gentleness of her disposition, and above all, her love for him, which was so apparent even in her despair But I could not calm him. --Ind ed he appeared to me to be disordered in his intellects ---I intreated him to compose himself, and assured him I would instantly write to you a whole account of his penitence and sufferings I attended him home, and prevailed on him to go to bed He made me relate to him all my conversation with you —And I believe would have detained me the whole night had I not reminded him of my intention of writing —he then hurried me from him

Thus, my charming Miss Vere, have I executed your commission Need I intreat you to use all your influence with your lovely friend to compassionate poor Darnley? yet has she not a more powerful advocate in her own bosom? I sincerely hope she has —He truly deserves pity. What a complicated scene of villainy has been found!

Believe me, madam, tho' never a professed libertine, I am become a sincere proselite to virtue · I ever admired, but now am resolved to practise it,

I am, with the truest esteem,
Madam,
your ever devoted,

HENRY CLAYTON

LETTER LXXXII

To Miss VERE

April 27

THIS moment I have perused the most tender epistle from the worthy Evelin He acquaints me me with his safe arrival, and his having learnt Lord L is at Lisle, whither he requests I will write to him. but I will enclose it, that you may see and admire his noble heart as I do

I have said every thing to quiet the tender suspicions his unfeigned affection suggests, and repeated my solemn resolution of being only his The person who brought me the letter was to take mine, as he came to England upon urgent business, which dispatched, he returns immediately

I do not doubt but in a little time I shall be quite reconciled to my lot, which half the world would envy There always seemed a bar between Sir George Darnley and me, we were not born for each other ---I am more and more convinced of it ---There likewise seems a great similarity of sentiment subsisting in Sir John Evelin and your Caroline ---heaven grant it may ever remain so!

However, my dear Sidney, I am not so strong yet, or have I so great an opinion of my fortitude, as to believe I could bear any great shock, therefore do not---I think you had better not, if you should hear from Colonel Clayton, do not communicate any thing to me, which may cause my resolution to waver ---For if you were only to say "he is convinced" those three little words would cause more emotion in my heart, than the wife of Sir Evelin ought to experience for any other man Does not that amiable man deserve every attention I can pay him?---And yet Sidney, shall I dare own it to you---it is the last pang of expiring weakness I could hardly sign my name to the assurances I gave Sir John Evelin, that my hand should be his whenever he claimed it A tear dropped on the paper, and a trembling seized the hand destined to him alone I strive, indeed I do to love him with my whole heart, but he has kindly given me time do you not then, my dearest friend, precipitate me. I am interrupted---The woman of the house tells me a lady wants to see me immediately, having something to communicate I wonder who it is, but I must be gone. I tremble---every thing puts me in a flutter

---

Almighty heaven protect and guide me! Teach me, O God, to endure this heavy conflict—Oh, Sidney, what a visitor—what a trial have I had!—Strengthen thy afflicted servant, O Lord, and keep me firm—Yet how can I be just to both? O that my death could end the cruel struggle!——But let me explain myself with some accuracy—I put up my writings, and went into the dining-room, on entering I heard in well-known sounds, "Where, where is the dear creature?" and the next moment Miss Harriet Darnley was in my arms——"Can you, can you forgive me," sobbed the dear girl, O my dearest, injured Caroline, can you forgive your cruel enemies?" I stared wildly—I was all confused.—Then pressing her to my bosom, Do I then hold my much loved friend? And are you at length convinced of my innocence? Gracious powers, is it possible!———

"Dear Caroline, I hate myself for ever, suspecting you, nor shall I cease to do so 'till you say you have freely forgiven me"

"Witness, heaven, with what rapture I receive you I can make great allowances for your conduct—But to what blest means do I owe this happiness?"

"My unhappy, too credulous brother, was at length undeceived by the interposition of Colonel Clayton—He besought me on his knees to fly to you.

you—I made all the inquiries I could, and now I have found you, we will never part again No we will never part.—You must, dearest Caroline, you must indeed pardon the sincerest penitent that ever stood in need of forgiveness my poor brother lives but in that hope, and were you to know the vile artifices which were practised to blacken your fame, you would less condemn erring mortals for giving belief to them you would, I am sure, be induced to receive to your favor my unhappy brother, tho' he used you unkindly"

'Ah, my dear Harriet, I have been hardly used, but I cease to remember it—If my forgiveness is necessary to your brother's happiness, it is not my nature to refuse it to him"

"Dear creature you make me happy I am sure" She flew to the door, and the next instant Sir George Darnley was at my feet The surprize was too great—Joy, and a thousand conflicting passions overcame me—The tender assiduity of persons so dear to me, presently recovered me—"I cannot, dare not hope to be forgiven," said the dear repentant Darnley "No, all angel as you are, altho' I heard the dear sounds from your lips—His voice was interrupted by tears and sobs—"O, my Caroline! once I might call you mine, can you look with compassion on a wretch like me?---Does not your soul abhor me?"

"Ah, Sir George!---could you ever accuse me of cruelty? I consider the treatment I have met with as only offered to the vile wretch you believed me to be—I condemn you not, or will I make a retrospect of what may recal scenes we wish to forget Rise then, my dear Sir George, and rise happy if my pardon can make you so" He pressed my hand to his lips, while Harriet took the other---"Dear amiable girl," said she, "how can I repay the ineffable delight you have given me, in

raising

raising my poor desponding brother to life and hope."

She related many circumstances of the diabolical arts of the vile Miss Grafton---I no longer wonder at their discarding me with infamy---I inquired after my dear good Mrs Grafton, thank God, she is well. She is now at the castle.

The hours slipt away imperceptibly, finding it near dinner time, I begged they would partake of my repast---Sir George took my hand, and with looks of the truest love, said, "Will my beloved Caroline add one more favor to those conferred on her happy Darnley—to quit these lodgings, and accompany us to St James's-Square?"

"Aye, do, my sweet girl," said Harriet.

O, Sidney, will you credit me,—so lost was I in rapturous joy, I had forgotten every engagement—each vow registered in heaven, 'till that request awakened me from my trance of happiness to real misery---They waited impatiently for my answer. a flood of tears was all I could give. I threw myself back in my chair, and covered my face with my handkerchief. "Ah! what do I see?—What mean these tears?" they both exclaimed—When I could speak, "Alas! why, why have I seen you? or why did I suffer a too transporting extasy to rob me of all recollection? Oh!—Darnley! we must part! I fear for ever---I cannot, cannot trust myself with another interview."

"Gracious heaven!" exclaimed he, almost frantic. "What is it I hear! Part did you say? ---O my adorable! my once kind love, on my knees I implore you to have compassion on my bleeding heart, and tell me how I may avert the dreadful curse you threaten me with? It cannot be that you wish to torture me; no, those streaming eyes and heart bursting sighs, are not indications of so cruel a purpose. What power then can part us? Are you not mine?—Punish me,—protract---delay my

happiness

happiness---But O my angelic Caroline, say not we must part!"——

"Witness for me heaven!" said I, lifting up my swimming eyes and hands, witness for me, O God! who seest the agony of my soul, what I feel on this trying conflict---O, Darnley, I can never be yours ---Fatally, too fatally have I vowed to be another's vowed beyond the power of retraction. Judge by your own what are my sufferings---Words are too weak to express them---Were you, Sir George, --were you, my Harriet, to know each circumstance, then would you see and allow there never was so ill-fated a wretch as the poor Caroline. But however miserable I am---I must, ---I will be just. I beg your assistance, beg your pity and compassion, ---for O, much I need them." Taking the letter I had received that morning from my pocket, I put it into the hand of Miss Darnley, "Read, read this, my dear Harriet----I cannot.----- But yet I will beg you to wait 'till I relate part of the affair." I then informed them in what a situation Sir John Evelin discovered me, and of his former attachment to me---His generosity which prompted him, tho' the world was against me, to be my friend, the manifold obligations I owed him, my belief that Sir George Darnley was inflexible in his resolution not to be convinced, and my knowledge that he was engaged to wed another——that other my greatest persecutor —— how was I to act?— What would you advise me to---You see the true state of the case. Can I plant daggers in the breast of a man who has risked all to serve me,---and yet can I make such a sacrifice? Heaven only knows the agonies of my soul on this occasion."

"Consent, my dear Sir George. Ah, how dear! to hear the letter."

"It is enough that I know myself wretched," cried he, in all the torture of despair? "what do the

the circumstances avail? You,---Oh! can I call you cruel,---you have pronounced my doom but I cease to complain Ah, wherefore should I She only who could give relief to my bursting heart, is she who pierced it"——

"Ah! you ought not to condemn me Think on my sufferings, think what I have endured since I was driven with disgrace from your house---Think what was my situation, nor wonder that I embraced the only asylum offered me in my distressed circumstances but, Oh, that I had not, but wayward fate, ever my attendant, impelled me to marry"

"But yet, Sir John Evelin, should he know your prior engagement might be induced"———

"Ah! read his letter——O! that you had ever remained in ignorance of my innocence ——or that I had seen you sooner Cursed, cursed delay, --but I was born to misery ——O Caroline, Caroline!" the tears fresh streaming from his eyes, "are you then cruelly resolved---must I be wretched? Is this indeed the last time my eyes must be blessed with thy beauties!——Must we part?——O, that they were closed for ever, since they must no longer look on thee"

"Would to heaven I were this moment expiring In my death alone can my sorrows cease Either way I must be wretched, but no thing shall shake my resolution of being just—I may be wretched, but I will not merit it Since we must part, why do we protract our separation"

"And can I, can I part with thee ---thou most amiable, most lovely of thy sex? My eyes may lose the blessing of beholding thee, but never, never shall my heart cease to think of thee"

"Yes, my dear Darnley, you must endeavor to forget I was ever dear to you Still think me unworthy of your esteem"

" Recover your peace of mind, and give me the only conſolation my wretched boſom now can taſte, the aſſurance of your not being unhappy

" Forget your Caroline! Then may heaven ſhower down its heavieſt curſes,---curſes yet un thought of, &c,'---and he kneeled down, " if ever one moment paſſes without your loved idea being fixed in my breaſt I ſwear to wear out the remainder of my days in mourning your loſs, and when I ceaſe to cheriſh you in my memory, may heaven make me more wretched, if poſſible, than I am. This inſtant, in parting from all my ſoul holds dear. ——You, my Harriot, may behold the lovely charmer, it is I, I alone am to be deprived of that felicity" He then approached me, who was almoſt a ſtatue, yet too feelingly alive to my diſtreſs —— " We muſt part then"——I anſwered but by my ſobs ——" This ſurely the happy Evelin would not deny me at our final ſeparation ——Oh death! what art thou, if thou exceedeſt this pang" He preſſed me almoſt lifeleſs to his boſom, and breaking forth into freſh agonies of grief, hurried from me I ſunk on the breaſt of Harriot, and gave myſelf up to the moſt exquiſite anguiſh. Me-thought my ſoul [illegible] left me ——I will not tire you with a repetition of my fruitleſs lamentations ——The poor Harriot too ——She ſtayed with me about two hours Soon after ſhe left me, ſhe ſent this little billet

" My unhappy brother has this inſtant left London He knows not whither he means to go, in ſearch of loſt repoſe. where alas! can he find it ——O Caroline! how are his pleaſing proſpects in this day over-blown, but I need not add to your diſtreſs, a greater pang, by expatiating on [illegible] loſt [illegible] Adieu ——I will be with you to morrow-morning"

No, Harriot,——you need not add to my diſtreſs indeed!——Already does it over-whelm me ——

Merciful

Merciful God! what a ſacrifice do I make of my love, and I fear eternal happineſs! Look round the world, and point out three beings more wretched --- Poor Darnley thou muſt for ever loſe the woman thy ſoul doated on!——Thy former errors are forgotten,---the remembrance of thy ſufferings alone remain——And muſt thy virtue, conſtancy and truth, moſt amiable Evelin, be beſtowed on one incapable, thro' never-ending miſeries of rewarding thy worth? And thou---wretched Caroline!---thou ſport of adverſe fortune! Muſt ſtill the peaceful haven of content be ever ſnatched from thy eager eyes, when thou haſt juſtly attained the view?

O Sidney, theſe trials are too great,——The divine hand alone which chaſtens me, can ſupport me through this vale of tears——O that I had paſſed it——and that it might be ſaid——Such were the ſufferings of the unfortunate

CAROLINE MELMOTH.

LETTER LXXXIII.

To Miſs VERE.

April 28.

ALAS! my Sidney, how cruelly did every thing conſpire to render my miſery complete! This morning Harriot came to me,—She ran into my arms—We neither of us could ſpeak,—but wept a conſiderable time—At length ſhe told me, of the unhappy ſtate in which poor Darnley left his houſe—She begged my permiſſion to apprize Sir John Evelin of every circumſtance——Ah! could I with honor comply with her requeſt?——Would justice prompt such proceedings?——My distresses are unparalleled, but still I will be just.

After some time I made inquiries of the rest of the family. Miss Darnley told me her sister was married on such a day [Ah, Sidney, on that day I remember seeing Frederic with a wedding favor in his hat,—that too contributed to the fatal promise] to Lord Wilton.

I said I had heard of the death of Lady Wilton, and sincerely congratulated the happy pair, on a union that promised so much felicity: adding, I had been acquainted with Lord Wilton's attachment to Louisa, before he left England.

"So we found" said Harriot, "tho' then we did not think so——My sister will be impatient to see you, and intreat your pardon for injuring you by her suspicions."

"Injuring me, my dearest Harriot! Ah, there was sufficient room to think me guilty!"

"You mistake me, my dear Caroline! but to render myself more clear, I must go back a little. Lady Wilton had long been very sensible of her Lord's merit."

"Who could know Lord Wilton and not do so."

"True, my Caroline: but every one is not affected alike by merit, however conspicuous. In short, Louisa was far gone in the passion of love, when she only thought she was giving way to an esteem she took a secret pleasure in indulging, 'till the assiduity Lord Wilton paid you, gave rise to emotions, which convinced her she not only was in love, but jealous likewise. Yet she thought,——what right have I to be displeased with Miss Melmoth?—Am I to prescribe rules to Lord Wilton—is he not to seek his happiness where he thinks he has the surest prospect of finding it? She saw, she acknowledged your transcendent merit, and the sentiment, which caused her admiration of you, made

her

ler at the ſame time ſuſceptible to the perfections of Lord Wilton His partiality to you was keenly obſerved by Louiſa ,—he was ever at your ſide : his behaviour to my ſiſter was conſtrained—he frequently would quit her abruptly—or be ſilently reſtleſs in her company , while to you he was all himſelf

" She was one day ear-witneſs to part of a converſation between his Lordſhip and you —What he ſaid convinced her, he was paſſionately in love , your anſwers were ſuch as evinced your great eſteem for him, mingled with pity These circumſtances ſhe kept intirely to herſelf —You remarked the alteration in her behavior —It is inconceiveable what ſhe ſuffered

" Had Lord Wilton felt a mutual paſſion, ſtill Louiſa would have found much in herſelf to condemn,—but as the preſent caſe was, how much to be blamed—how much to be pitied ſhe thought herſelf !

" When my brother declared his attachment to you, ſhe could not conceal her aſtoniſhment, on hearing you profeſſed a partiality She thought you ſelf-intereſted in accepting the hand of Sir George, becauſe ſhe deemed it impoſſible for any woman beloved by, and loving Lord Wilton, to feel a paſſion for any other , for ſhe had not the leaſt doubt of ſome ſecret engagement between his Lordſhip and you, which to her, juſtified your former rejection of Davenport

" Miſs Grafton's treachery againſt you ſoon followed my brother's declaration —My ſiſter then ſaw you in the moſt deſpicable light of a vile mercenary —She acquainted my mother and me with her ſentiments concerning you and Lord Wilton —Nothing was too bad to be believed of you —We joined in diſſuading Sir George from ſo vile an union.—Louiſa was moſt violent, ſhe felt herſelf

 injured .

injured what said she, not content with encouraging the addresses of a married man, and carrying on a shameful intrigue with another, but at the same time endeavoring to draw in the heir of an ancient house, to conceal her enormities? Such, my dear Caroline, from the machinations of the infamous Grafton, and her vile associate, were the bitter reflections cast on the most amiable and most injured of women."

"When a person is going down the hill of adversity, every little push helps to precipitate them still lower.—Every one lent their hand to throw you from the summit you had gained."

"What my sister alledged against you had great weight with my brother, and if it was not the principal circumstance which irritated him against you, it yet laid open his heart to receive every ill impression.—How fatally all things succeeded to render so many unhappy!

"The news of Lady Wilton's death reached us. It caused some emotions in the breast of Louisa.

"We went all to Darnley Grove, except Sir George.---Indeed we saw very little of him while in town. He hurried into any company to drive your idea, if possible, from his mind.---One day on making some alteration in the chamber which was appropriated to your use while with us, part of the furniture was taken out of the room. My sister's maid pulled out the drawers of a bureau, in order to move it with more ease, behind one of them she found a letter directed to you. Louisa and I were in the dressing-room.---Here ladies, said Betty, a letter of Miss Melmoth's.---O burn it, cried Louisa, do not let any thing remain to remind us of that creature.---Let us first peruse it rejoined I, perhaps it may throw some light on her very mysterious conduct. Saying which, I took the letter, and running my eye over it, saw it subscribed Wilton,

I gave

I gave it without further notice to my sister I saw a visible change in her countenance---she trembled, and almost breathless flung herself into a chair -- Heavens! exclaimed I, what can be the contents of this letter? You ought not, my dear Louisa, to suffer any further knowledge of the abandoned girl's baseness thus to affect you It contains a confirmation, I suppose, of her affair with Lord Wilton, but that you before suspected O that she was as innocent of all other crimes as this letter proves her of that! see, my dear Harriet, presenting it to me Never did astonishment equal mine"

" Good God! exclaimed Louisa, how have I injured both her and Lord Wilton!—Poor unhappy, infatuated Caroline! how I long to ask thy pardon---Ah, that thou couldst prove thyself equally injured by all thy accusers! her joy in finding herself beloved by the only man that ever touched her heart, like Aaron's rod, swallowed up every other consideration, which, may perhaps, in a little, excuse a conduct, I fear not wholly laudable---Yet when we reflect dispassionately on the affair---our earnest desire of seeing the best of brother's restored to peace of mind and happiness---this, only clearing you of the most trivial of your faults—all these considerations may, I think, circumstanced as we were, exculpate us in our resolution of not making Sir George acquainted with this event

" In a few weeks, Lord Wilton wrote to Lady Darnley and Louisa, intreating their permission to return and ratify a passion he had long cherished, but dared not before avow from the perplexing circumstances he then laboured under, but from which he was now happily disengaged He referred for the sincerity of his passion, to you, whom he said had been the faithful confidante of his attachment to Miss Darnley

"My mother scrupled not shewing these letters to Sir George, from a conviction he had now conquered his ill-placed passion, but the emotion plainly discovered the command you had still over him. Desirous of seeing the happiness of our beloved brother regained, we daily pressed him to marry; he at length, consented to our wishes, or rather ceased to refuse us. But as to making any choice, he was, he said, totally incapable, he would leave it to us. He should never again know happiness, [illegible] to him, with whom he [illegible]—All women were now alike to him."

"We named Miss Grafton to him, being of a family and fortune equal to his own. He silently acquiesced to our proposal. The affair seemed chiefly managed by Lady Darnley and Mrs Grafton. Sir George took very little pleasure in the company of his mistress—in short, he was totally changed from the agreeable entertaining man we once knew him, and the reflection of who was the cause of such an alteration, exasperated us still more against you."

"My mother was desirous of having the marriage of Sir George and Louisa celebrated at the same time. My brother still made no objection. He frequently said his heart could never know [illegible] love, but that his life, or the circumstances of it, were of so little concern to him, that he could not think he paid his friends any great compliment when he left the disposal of it to them."

"After being out one night, which I have since learnt, was when he rescued you from the fire, he [illegible], which proved a very dangerous fever. He, however, breathed not a complaint—[illegible] Louisa's marriage might be concluded [illegible] at the appointed time."

Sir George recovered well enough to be preſent at the ceremony, and to attend the bride-folks into the country."

"Lady Wilton was deſirous of having us to ſtay ſome time with her, but Sir George was impatient to return to town: my mother hoped it proceeded from his wiſh of being near Miſs Grafton."

"Lord and Lady Wilton jointly preſſed my mother to continue with them. I therefore accompanied Sir George to St. James's-Square."

"Still he continued reſtleis and uneaſy, but the affair with Miſs Grafton went on, and a day was named. We were to ſpend the evening in Groſvenor-Square, but a note being brought my brother, he begged me to make his excuſe, and went out, as he ſaid, to meet Colonel Clayton."

"When I came home at night, I found Sir George in the deepeſt diſtreſs—Anguiſh was painted on his countenance—But it is needleis to dwell on this ſubject—we uſed every endeavor to diſcover your retreat—at laſt we ſucceeded.—The reſt is too well known to you.—Ah, my dear Caroline, how I regret—how ſhall I ever regret the not informing Sir George at firſt, when we found Lord Wilton's letter to you.—Or, had you intruſted Louiſa with his ſecret paſſion—but fate ſeemed to pre-ordain this cruel affair."

"Ah!" cried I, weeping, "every thing conſpired to make me wretched."

"And not you alone, my ſweet friend.—my poor brother."

"Heaven reſtore him to happineſs, and enable me to ſupport the heavy taſk aſſigned me! Ah, Evelin, what a ſacrifice I make thee!—but it muſt be ſo."——

April 29.

Mrs and Miss Grafton are, I find, in the country, whither they went, when Sir George declined visiting them. He had not been able to enter into particulars with Mrs Grafton, only informed her in a polite manner, that it would be impossible to effect an union between their families.

I had not spirits or inclination to ask Miss Dorley many questions, or, indeed, was she capable of answering.

Sincerely she loves her brother. Great Heaven! and must I cease to love him?—Must I forget him? Even when I thought him cruel, unjust, ungrateful, still I loved him, and now---Ah! must I tear him from my heart! drive his long-loved image from that heart, which beats but for him -- Give my vows to another? -- Must another claim all my tenderness---all my love? --My esteem is his ---can I grant him more?---I cannot bestow my heart, tho' I sacrifice to him every prospect of happiness ---Yet he deserves it all --Best of men, [illegible] ould'st thou pity me, how much I merit the pity of the whole world!

May 2.

I lament my hard fortune, perhaps with greater energy, than many others would. Half the world would not see my misfortunes, in the light I behold them. But is not misery great in proportion to our feelings of it? It is not in misfortunes themselves, [illegible] but

but in the manner of our bearing them, we suffer. If I am more deeply affected by these repeated strokes of distress, than another would be in the same predicament, does it argue I feel less pain?— surely not

How often, since thus I have been familiar with grief in the several gradations of it, have I exclaimed, my heart was broken! I could not support it! Either our hearts are not composed of perishable materials, or grief cannot kill, for I am still living to lament [fruitless lamentation] ills, which had any one told me, I could have survived, would hardly have gained my belief.

Ah, why do we congratulate ourselves on our boasted reason and knowledge, above our fellow creatures! Is happiness the consequent companion of knowledge and reason? Alas! too frequently we find these envied qualities, the source of our ills in life Too deep reasoning has often destroyed the felicity we might else---had we been blessed with ignorance, have tasted Of what use then is knowledge to us short-sighted mortals,---unless it could teach us to avoid the path which leads to sorrow?--- We see, indeed, the shoals, the quicksands, the rocks, the precipices, from the gift of boasted knowledge, we know life is subject to these, and many other casualties, but we are incapable of guarding against, or extricating ourselves from, when involved in them

Had I remained in a state of happy ignorance, I should never have gained the heart, or even engaged the attention of the most lovely of men,--- forgive me, Evelin, if I this once stile him so--- My heart would then have been incapable of receiving either pain or pleasure, from the passion of love --- I had not then been the object of malice or envy I should not now be lamenting miseries, which my ignorance would have sheltered me from,

but

but then I ſhould have been inſenſible, to the dear delight, that friendſhip affords Ah! that I could have remained ſatisfied with that ſentiment alone! Why was my heart capacious enough to admit another partner? Ah, my deareſt Sidney, friend of my ſoul! why didſt thou not reign ſolely in that heart?—What pain, what anguiſh, would then have been ſaved me Cruel deſtructive paſſion! how art thou degenerated! Intereſt—Interrupted—A pacquet—Ah! my God, from whom? my deſtined—Sidney! my pen refuſes to trace the fatal—O pity your unhappy friend—never did I need it more—A fortnight hence—Ah, he will be here—Then I muſt—Oh, heavens! I muſt—I tremble—I can no longer hold my pen.

I cannot tranſcribe the fatal letter My tears have almoſt obliterated each trace of the tendereſt effuſion of that moſt generous man Ah! why have I not a heart? Unworthy, as I am, muſt I be inſenſible too?

I am not well—My nerves are ſhattered—every noiſe makes me ſtart, and I turn haſtily to the door again, O! my God! I expected comfort to enter The good Johnſon aſks eagerly what I want, what would my deareſt young lady have? Her eyes red with weeping—Ah what would I have!—that is a queſtion I dare not reſolve.——

I will ſend you the letter, when Miſs Darnley has ſeen it—that dear kind girl is now come

Adieu,

CAROLINE MELMOTH

LETTER

LETTER LXXXIV.

To Miſs MELMOTH.

Dijon

WITH what heart-felt ſatisfaction I acquaint the moſt amiable of women, Lord L. is willing to do juſtice to her merit

In my laſt, I informed you I heard where Lord L was I diſpatched a meſſenger to him, importing my deſire of waiting on his Lordſhip, and intimated my buſineſs He returned for anſwer, he was to be met with at ſuch a place, where, what he had dared to act, he dared juſtify, his menace gave me very little concern.

I went to him and introduced myſelf At firſt he treated me very cavalier, but when he found he had a man to encounter, incapable of fear, he a little altered his carriage

" The buſineſs we have to diſcuſs, Sir John, may be ſoon ſettled "

" It may, my Lord, and in what manner you pleaſe "

" You are the knight-errant I find, Sir John, who have eſpouſed the cauſe of injured innocence" —" And who, romantic as it may ſound, my Lord," interrupting him, " to a man of your principles, am determined in defence of that injured Lady's cauſe, to loſe the laſt drop of my blood "

" *Fort gallant* faith ! but a Lady of Miſs Melmoth's beauty, will never want a champion "

" A Lady of Miſs Melmoth's virtue will never want a champion, while there is a man of honor exiſting, who has reſolution to chaſtiſe a villain, tho' a titled one "

Perhaps I exceeded the bounds of politeneſs here His Lordſhip expreſſed violent diſpleaſure. but the ſneer

ſneer with which he ſpoke the laſt words, threw me off my guard.

I coolly ſaid, "My Lord, the man who is unconſcious of deſerving the character of villain, will never be offended at hearing there are ſuch. Your Lordſhip would excite ſuſpicions, in any one who did not know you. I am come, my Lord, thus far, to demand a juſtification of actions, the moſt cruel ever perpetrated—the blaſting the character of the moſt innocent and virtuous of women—The motive to it, her impregnable virtue."

"You came to argue then, Sir John—to reaſon. —I have not ſupplied myſelf with words;—this way lies my argument," laying his hand on his ſword.—"Here,—Evelin, you ſhall find me a man of honor."

"You talk of honor, my Lord, permit me to ſay you miſtake the meaning of the word.—You ſaid, what you dared do, you dared juſtify; that is your definition of honor. You have done an ill action,—Your Lordſhip is a man of too much modern gallantry, to bluſh at owning an ill action—and you would juſtify it by taking my life, or loſing your own."

"Honor, my Lord, is a ſacred thing; it conſiſts in actions conformable to reaſon. St. Evremond was the beſt judge of it, of any man in the world. If, ſays he, honor conſiſts alone in courage, a man of honor would make a contemptible figure oppoſed to a ruſſian bear. I never doubted your Lordſhip's courage, but your honor muſt with me remain queſtionable, while you decline doing juſtice to an unhappy, injured, virtuous woman.—Can you aſſume that ſacred character, when you reflect that thro' your means, and by your practices, one of the moſt lovely and amiable of her ſex, is rendered miſerable?—cut off from the pleaſing proſpects ſhe had a right to indulge,—deprived of friends,—repu-

tation

tation blasted,—wounded in the estimation of the man she loved?—given up to a life of tears—and by whom? Can honor warm the breast of such a man?"

"O, my Lord let reason convince you; attend to her calls. Suffer the small still voice of conscience to awaken justice and honor in your soul."

"I much fear, my Lord, you never experienced the heart-felt satisfaction attending a good action. —Why will you deprive yourself of one of the noblest pleasures man can taste? It behoves you to make all the atonement in your power for the injuries you have done Miss Melmoth. But I will reason with you more like a man of the present world. What advantage has the ruin of this amiable Lady's reputation been of to you? You find you went upon a very mistaken principle, if you thought that to render yourself the worst of enemies to Miss Melmoth, was the road to her heart. But perhaps the possession of her heart was not the object, Good God! is it possible that any man could feel a passion for so divine a creature, and not wish a return?"

"Sweet are the joys which come with willingness," is a sentiment in the mouths of libertines.

"Possibly you thought [vainly, as you found it] that when deprived of every hope—every wish broken in upon, every chance of happiness vanished, she would, having no other alternative, fly for succor to the man by whom, every hope, every innocent wish, every chance of happiness was destroyed!'

'Ask your own heart, my Lord, if it has received any recompense in the accomplishment of this work, which will compensate for the anguish you will one day endure on this account? In pity to an injured lovely woman,—in pity to yourself, act the

the part of a man of honor, and receive the highest reward—A self applauding conscience"

"I could add still further arguments, but, I hope, they would be needless—Were you to listen to the dictates of your heart, I think they would"

"I will own to you, Sir John, which yet I never did to any man, I took some pains to gain Miss Melmoth, perhaps you, dull honest fellows, might stile them dishonorable Stratagems I used, which you know is allowable, both in love and war Force, I ever abhorred, it was contrary to my nature, which never wanted a stimulus in my affairs with the women But after such a concession, I think I have a right to demand the nature of your connexion with Miss Melmoth"

I frankly owned, I lived but in the hope of calling you mine. For a long time he would not relinquish his claim, as he called it, to you he swore no one but yourself could repay him all he had suffered, nor could any one make you amends, but him I at last convinced him of the absurdity of his hopes, and he consented to my proposal, provided I would give him my word, that you would freely pardon him: my proposition was, that he should write a full and true account of his and his vile emissary's plots against you, which I might shew to Mrs Grafton

Thus, my adorable Caroline, have I accomplished the task you honored me with Now will the scruples of the most delicate of minds be obviated, to ease that mind, did I undertake this journey

What bliss I feel at the thoughts of soon being with you! That time would have been very soon, but for a little affair, I have it in my power to transact for a worthy man in great distress, tho' unsolicited I could not refuse my assistance, happy as I am in prospect, to faciliate every one's happiness, as far as I can.

I have

I have just perused your dear welcome epistle, how has it encreased my love, admiration and gratitude! Before, they seemed to know no bounds. Ah! should any envious demon interpose to rob me of my Caroline, it would be impossible for me to support it.—But wherefore these doubts? Has not the most amiable of women owned her esteem, her exalted friendship?—Is she not mine by the strongest ties? should any thing happen to deprive me of the place I at present hold in your esteem, and to dash my hopes, my constant prayer to heaven is, that I may die here, and think you mine.—I would not resign my hopes for universal empire. In less than a fortnight, from this time, my lovely Caroline may expect her highly obliged, and ever faithful

JOHN EVELIN.

LETTER LXXXV.

To Miss MELMOTH.

Vere-Park, May 3.

MY acquaintance with Lady Betty Cranford has been productive of two or three interesting circumstances.

The embarras I met with there yesterday, has given rise to some reflections, not altogether so pleasing.

I know not what to think.—However, I will not retard your knowledge of the event by any animad-

versions

versions of my own, but without further prel... will inform you, there was a ball given at Crau... manor, on the birth day of its worthy possess... I of course was invited.

I dressed myself suitable to the occasion, a... the people I was to meet. Women love to ... upon trifles, and to make them matters of consequence, a remark of a he-creature: but notwithstanding that sage remark is before my eyes, I must tell you how I was drest. In the first place, a white and silver negligee, without a hoop, as I think it altogether impertinent in a woman to incommode a whole assembly with the enormous ... of a whale. Why should not the men assume a privilege, to which they have undoubtedly an equal right, to wear their swords? I wish the men would enter into an association never to ask any woman to dance country dances in a hoop.—But I forgot all this time I am only in my negligee.—On my head I wore a little spangled hood, on one side, turban-wise,—but it will take up too much time to enumerate every article of my dress; I think it is a flagrant proof of our sex's fondness of it, that they do not forget some or other of the various parts of it. My contested jewels too were all put on in an elegant stile, so that like me *tout-ensemble*, I was, if you will give me the credit, I gave my glass no very despicable figure.

When the labors of the toilet were over I fluttered down stairs, swam into the drawing room where I knew my sweet step-dame was, and humming an Italian air, surveyed my lovely form in the glass. When making a few alterations in my dress, asked her ladyship's advice on the important concern of placing a bunch of roses. I saw she was mortally offended at not being invited, and sensibly piqued at my trifling with her, for I professed prodigious concern that she must stay at home

home But the post chaise coming in the midst of my condolations, I wisked into it, and was bowled away to Crauford manor

I was introduced to Lady Betty, surrounded by Belles, she sat down by me Her ladyship told me, "Colonel Clayton had been invited, but was gone a little tour with Sir George Darnley, nothing else" added she, " would have prevented his being here, but I believe, we shall be able to procure you a partner "

" Why, was Colonel Clayton to have been the happy man ?

" Perhaps he might But wont you honor Lord Charles with your hand ?"

" You know I never care whom I dance with "

" My brother would be very unhappy, were he to hear you say so "

" Why then, Lady Betty, I am not quite so indifferent about dancing with Lord Charles, because he is your brother he has lately treated me with particularity. I would not trifle with so near a relation of yours, were he only an acquaintance, I might perhaps be induced to coquet a little, with so pretty a fellow "

" Well, then," smiling good humouredly, " you have thought proper to refuse me, but what will you say to Mr Crauford ?

" Am I so happy as to be the subject of your conversation ?" asked Mr Crauford, coming up to us with tickets for places, " but leave of trifling, and come to business "

" Here is a gentleman, my dear Miss Vere, who has been some time a stranger to you, will you take compassion on him ?"

" With all my heart, Mr. Crauford. I am at your service "

" I wish you was at the service of the man I shall

shall introduce to you" looking with great meaning.

"Who is he! I am all impatience, come, come, tell me quickly?"

Lady Betty laughed at my eagerness, but composing her features, said "It will be better to inform you of the arrival of a man, for whom you profess a great esteem. Mr Crauford wanted to surprise you, but, woman-like, I long to tell you."

"Upon my word, I feel myself interested in the affair. Do, my dear Lady Betty, unfold the mystery quite, and not, by shewing me part of the story, excite my curiosity still farther." But ere she could speak, the mystery unravelled itself, Mr. Crauford entered, with Mr Mordaunt in his hand, —he was in deep mourning. I underwent some emotion, which I fear my countenance betrayed—I don't know why, I did not expect him to be a stranger.—He knew he was to see me, yet he turned pale when he approached me.——I think his pining and grieving has not much altered him.—he made me some politer compliments than I thought I deserved, tho' Lady Betty told me before, that he had entirely forgot my ridiculous treatment of him. I returned them, not without hesitation, conscious of the inferiority of being once in the wrong.

After some time, he talked in a lively disengaged manner, that had an agreeable effect upon me, taking off that little troublesome sensation I at first laboured under.

We conversed on many topics, as he sat next me.

I looked with a scrutinizing eye round the room, to discover, if I could, Mr Mordaunt's Lady: there were four ladies in black, strangers to me, so that I could not be certain whether my search was attended with success. I thought it an awkward had queſtion to aſk him, and for ſome time de-liberated the propriety or not, of ſuch an interrogatory, at laſt, female curioſity, overcame my more back-ward ſcruples, and I ventured to pop the queſtion ; tho' I could not directly ſay, " which is your wife ?" the word would not ſlip glibly off my tongue —and yet few give any trouble to me

" I have employed my eyes ſome time. to find out which is the ſovereign lady of your heart I ſup-poſe ſhe is here."

" Yes," anſwered he, with ſomething like a half-ſmothered ſigh, " the lovely woman, whom I muſt ever adore, is, as you ſuppoſe, madam, here "

" I pray," ſaid I ſmiling, " direct my eyes to the lovely woman "

" I will ſhew you her picture, and from the like-neſs, you will diſcover the moſt charming creature in the world

[Thankleſs man, thought I, you might have ex-cepted the company, if you were ever ſo fond of your wife]

" My dear Lady Betty, " continued Mr Mor-daunt, " will you favor me with that little box, I had the honor to preſent to you yeſterday."

She gave him a very handſome one, mounted with gold and enamelled He opened it, and placed it before my eyes I was juſt going to ex-claim, a lovely woman indeed ! but luckily for me, I diſcovered my miſtake —Will you believe it, in the lid of the box—deuce take it, was a ſmall con-vex mirror It is morally impoſſible to expreſs to you my feelings, becauſe yet I cannot find an aſſem-blage of words adequate to them I had power to ſhut the treacherous lid, and returning it to Mr. Mordaunt, ſaid, " I expected a little more ſince-rity from you, Sir, but ſind you have learnt from the jeſuits, during your long reſidence with them, to to evade giving a plain anſwer to a natural queſtion.

“Ah! madam! do me not the injuſtice to think me inſincere, ſince I only ſpoke [illegible] that he—”

“—[illegible] too,” interrupting him, a little recovered from [illegible] into which his [illegible] had [illegible] me, ‘indeed, you are become a great proficient.’

‘I [illegible] under your apprehension I conde[illegible] [illegible] of a paſſion, which has e[illegible] all my [illegible]

“You ought to conſider, Sir,” ſaid I, looking very grave, “any intimation of that nature, muſt be unſeaſonable from you. I did not, indeed, expect this levity from a man of Mr Mordaunt's ſentiments—ſo oppoſite to my knowledge, and eſtimation of his former character: however, Sir, as Mr Crauford has injudiciouſly adjudged us partners for the evening, we will, if you pleaſe, join the dancers.”

I felt myſelf diſpleaſed—mortified—and lowered—I knew not how I danced, or any thing about it. My head was filled with ſuch ſelf-humiliating reflections.—To my former ridiculous conduct, muſt I aſcribe theſe unpardonable freedoms. He left me a coquet—he expected to find me ſuch;——and conſequently liſten with avidity, to the profeſſions of love, from any man——I could not enter into the ſpirit of gaiety, which almoſt generally preſided: nor did my partner——He treated all the ladies, in mourning, with the ſame indifference, which I now ſcrupled not to attribute to his being become quite a modern huſband.

I own, on the firſt of our converſation, I was almoſt induced—if not to envy Mrs Mordaunt, yet, to think her a very happy woman, but now my ſentiments were totally changed, as indeed he ſeemed to be. I thought him greatly improved in

his

his person, but I thought, at the same time, were he as handsome as an angel, I had reason to congratulate myself on escaping him ——I sighed involuntarily, when I looked at him, that he should be so different from his former self · but I had charity enough to find an excuse—or at least what appeared so to me, tho' that turned my pity from him into displeasure, against your little Sidney I looked on myself as the primary cause of this change After his rencontre with Archer, and dismission from Vere-Park, he became quite unsettled ——careless and trifling ——Disappointed in his rational plan, might he not have fallen into bad company, whose follies and vices have made an impression not to be erased ——He trod the path of rectitude and honor,—in it he met disappointment, perhaps the path of pleasure were pointed out to him, by some dissolute companion, and the flowery entrance charmed him to pursue it this last reflection rendered me wholly incapable of attending to any thing I sat down, I could not divest myself of it Mr Mordaunt went to the other side of the room, where was Crauford talking to one of the ladies in mourning she made room between Crauford and herself for Mordaunt

That insufferable fop, Lord Charles, sat down by me, and employed his time in defeating his own purpose, if he meant to entertain me, as his conversation only served to disgust me —Is it impossible Lady Betty and he can be so nearly related ! In the midst of a fine poetical flourish of his,—for he does not always descend to prose, and never to common sense, I observed Mr Mordaunt chattering freely with the suspected lady,—to tell you the truth, my eyes had been rivetted almost to his chair —I hastily snapped the thread of his lordship's discourse, by asking him abruptly, who that lady was, Mr Mordaunt was then talking to ?

"Let

"Let me perish, if Mordaunt is not the happiest fellow in the universe, to have so divine a creature solicitous about him."

"Your lordship mistakes, it was the lady I was enquiring after."

"Ah, my adorable charmer! I have perceived your eyes ask Mordaunt that question several times."

"But, as I am not yet resolved, will you be so kind as to inform me? I take that Lady to be Mrs Mordaunt, am I mistaken?"

"Ha! ha! ha! laughed the insipid nobleman, to shew his white teeth, I suppose. That is immensely high, by Jupiter! Mrs Mordaunt!—No, faith! I hope we shall not see her here. Ha! ha! ha! I cannot but think how cursedly chagrin Mordaunt would be at such a rencontre."

"Oh! I shall expire at the idea!"

"I wish, my Lord, you would reduce your conversation to a little common sense, that I might have a chance of comprehending you. If there was any wit in what you said, I am either too dull to perceive it, or you destroyed it by laughing so immoderately. Pray, my lord, give me a plain rational answer."

"Well, madam," bowing, as if it was an easy matter for him to be rational,—"You now see before you, your most obsequious slave, who, as the sacred oracles of Delphi, is prepared to answer my lovely interrogatist."——

——"And will answer just as much to the purpose, I suppose: but I need not repeat my question."

"Curse catch me! if I am not immensely sorry to confess any word that falls from "that love-fraught lip," should not sink into the tables of my memory, but let me die, if I have not forgot every trace of the question."

"Well, my Lord, that you may not have the redundance

redundance of your wit to plead in excuse again, I will repeat my request, of being informed where Mrs Mordaunt is?

"Why, faith, my dear creature, she is neither here nor there.—I beg your pardon Miss Vere," seeing me assume an air of anger and contempt.—"She is gone a long journey."

"Mr Mordaunt has just taken one."

"Yes, but not with her. In short, she is gone into the country that Shakespear says something about."

"Your Lordship is a very proper representative of an oracle, I must confess."

"By my soul, I do not wonder I talk such cursed nonsense in your company."

I bowed. I am much obliged to Lord Charles C——

"Egad! I am still on the wrong side of the post. But you are so quick at repartee: I was going to say, that when in your company, I could think, nor talk of nothing but the effect of your charms."

"If it was possible for any thing to have effect on your Lordship, my inquiry would perhaps have been answered."

"Well then," said he, affectedly putting his chapeau bras before his eyes, now there is an opaque body between me and the sun, I will endeavor to satisfy your divine Ladyship's curiosity,—Mrs Mordaunt is deceased—absolutely dead."

"Dead!"

"Yes faith," twirling his hat on his hand, "she is dead."

"How long since?"

"Some few months.—Suddenly too, I heard, but"—yawning, "I always forget the circumstances of such dismal affairs."

Unfeeling wretch!——

My sentiments for Mr Mordaunt instantly

changed. Esteem again resumed its place Yet I could not alter my behavior to him I was fearful of giving rise to suspicions, had I treated him with greater freedom, now I knew he was a widower—Besides, I know not how, the same uneasy restraint I experienced at the first *rencontre* returned—I ſtill declined dancing, tho' Mr Mordaunt solicited me

Lord Charles said to him, in the most unfeeling manner, "Mordaunt, I have been acquainting Miss Vere with a few particulars of your private history

"She has not been much entertained then I fear"

"You have seen strange vicissitudes, Mr Mordaunt, since you left England!"

"I have indeed, Madam—and melancholy ones too, as I suppose his Lordship has informed you"

"Lord Charles only mentioned the greatest,—the last sad event"

"His happy Lordship feels not the woes of others—All are not blest with such insensibility"

"A blessing do you call it, Mr Mordaunt? sure, the not being capable of melting at another's woe must be the most horrid state in the world"

"You will then receive pain, Miss Vere, when you are acquainted with the sad story of my life, since I quitted England"

"It will yet be a pleasing melancholy, tho' our sympathizing sorrow can do no service."

"The pleasure of obeying you, madam, will be a sufficient inducement to me, to live over my griefs again, by committing them to paper"

I bowed, and thanked him

Just before I went away, Lady Betty told me, her brother, Lord Charles, had been very importunate with her, to intercede for him with me He had likewise bespoke Mr. Mordaunt's interest How can the Man be so absurd As the brother of Lady Betty, I have paid him some respect but as the trifling Lord Charles C I despise him

I menti-

I mentioned to Lady Betty, what Mr Mordaunt had said; she was vastly pleased, and told me I must communicate the whole to her, if I pleased.

Your affairs, my dearest Caroline, are, I think, in them, and will be happily settled, — I am impatient for a letter from you. — Behold, this moment the pacquet is come. This letter is sufficiently long. I will close it before I allow myself to open your's. —— Adieu!

SIDNEY VERE.

LETTER LXXXVI.

To Miss MILMOTH.

Vere-Park, May 6.

YOUR griefs, your distresses, my Caroline, are mine. My heart is too full to attempt a consolation. Sorrows, my love, are not hereditary, they are common to all.

I cannot write—but will send you the history of Mr Mordaunt. — In his life — But I will not another word—indeed, I am not capable.

Take this account in his own words. — In his grief, perhaps, you may, for a moment, forget your own.

After, Madam, I had met with the greatest of disappointments to all my fond wishes, England became hateful to me, and I determined to seek that happiness in a foreign land I had missed in my own.

But could I fly from myself? could I abstract my ideas from what I loved, and loving,—lamented?

Solitude, tho' it nourished my passion, I still preferred, or rather, was incapable of mixing in a crowd too happy to admit so forlorn a wretch as I was. I retired to a little village, a few miles from Lyons, living secluded from the world.

There I accidentally met a gentleman, to whom I had been of some service in England,—a native of Tholouse. He sought to repay it by the utmost attention. He would not suffer me to be alone. He dragged me into society.—A stranger to the frowns of fortune, he enjoyed her smiles without alloy. In short, he almost forced me to Paris, but I had resided there a long time, when on my travels, I still avoided seeing any thing.

At length, Monsieur de Montier prevailed on me to accompany him to Tholouse, where his family expected him.

We were received with great joy, by his father and mother, and two amiable sisters.

In this family I enjoyed a tranquillity I had long been unacquainted with. They were all polite, affectionate, and truly amiable. Both the sisters were charming women. The youngest professed great vivacity, mixed with the most winning softness.

"I have no patience," said she to me, one day, with the superiority which you men claim over our sex. You exclude us from traveling and learning, merely because you will keep us in subjection. I envy my brother—he has been in England, when he and you talk English how I dwell on the sounds. Why was I not a man?—Is it so very difficult a language?"

"Application, madam, and so good a capacity as you are blessed with, would soon make you a great proficient."

"I love England—I have read your history."

"Ay,"

"Aye," ſaid her brother, "ſhe loves England ſo much, that once ſinging ſome Engliſh words, ſhe ſet them to muſic, and uſed to ſing them. It was before I went to England, or knew any thing of the language; I fancy I ſhould laugh now at her pronunciation."

I offered to become her tutor; ſhe accepted me, and we devoted a part of every day to this avocation. What painful recollections did theſe taſks recal to my mind!—Ah! what hours were thoſe! What an employment mine, when I had the honor of perfecting you, madam, in the Italian! Why was I conſtrained to reſign it?

The train of thoughts which naturally occurred, deprived me of the peace I was juſt beginning to taſte. My amiable pupil obſerved the change. To eaſe my over charged heart one day, I made her partly the confidante of my unfortunate paſſion; but this *confidante* deſtroyed the innocent pleaſure we uſed to take in our ſtudies.—Lauriette was no longer the ſame; ſhe forgot her Engliſh to dwell on the diſtreſs of her tutor.—She did more; ſhe attempted to conſole him; but the indulgence of grief rather increaſes it.

At this time I left Tholouſe with young De Montier for ſome weeks.——When we returned, I was the firſt to diſcover an alteration in my pupil. "I am afraid," ſaid I to her, "you have forgot your leſſons. Have you purſued your ſtudies, with the aſſiduity you promiſed?—Or am I to find fault with you for neglect?"

"I begin to think," anſwered ſhe, with her eyes caſt down, "I have ſpent much idle time, in what can never be of uſe to me. I have therefore, and ſhall decline loſing more in acquiring, what I wiſh I had not attempted."

"From whence proceeds this reſolution, my

charming pupil?—Why," taking her hand, "would you deprive me of my scholar?"

She struggled her hand from mine. "Pray, Sir, don't take these freedoms.—I am not your pupil now." She soon after left the room, nor appeared again 'till supper.

We passed several days thus. They were to me very painful ones, as her conversation had been my chief happiness.

A relation of the family came to spend some weeks at the house. Mademoiselle St Hermoine, was of a temper and disposition to enliven all company: she would be for ever projecting some scheme of pleasure, and would extract happiness from every event in life. We all seemed possessed by the genius of chearfulness, except the little Laurette: she alone wore the appearance of discontent. She was disgusted with the vivacity of her cousin.—Every thing displeased her, who used before to give pleasure to, and receive it from, every body.

Sometimes, when I looked at her, I found her eyes fixed on me, she would hastily remove them, and on some pretence quit the room. This was extremely [illegible] to me. I was unconscious of having given her offence, and yet I could not but see, I was the object that gave her most uneasiness.

[illegible] de Monnier being absent, and Laurette de[illegible] [illegible] of our parties, De Montier, the [illegible] [illegible] Hermoine, and I were continually [illegible] about. I frequently complained to her of the [illegible] of her cousin to me, declaring I could [illegible] the reason. It seemed as if I was [illegible], and yet she used to treat me differently, [illegible] she could not behave politely to me herself, [illegible] that I should be in friendship with any [illegible]

St Hermoine said, she found her very much altered, she was always particularly fond of her, but now affected to take no notice of her; in short, her whole system of behavior consisted in contradictions From one of the sweetest dispositions, she became fretful, peevish, and ill-tempered.

Mademoiselle St Hermoine prepared to leave us —Two days before her departure, I asked her permission to be her escorte

"Certainly," said she, "you only mean this as a compliment. How well fitted you would be, if I was to take you at your word"

"You may, indeed If you won't accept of my services, I cannot help it, but do not question my veracity"

"Sure you won't leave us?" said Madame de Montier, "I have so long looked on you as part of the family, that I shall not be able to consent to your departure."

"Not to accompany Mademoiselle your niece?"

"I wish," said old Montier, "she had such a guard for life."

I bowed —"What say you, madam," taking both her hands, "will you admit me for your perpetual escorte?"

"Let me see how you behave on trial, before I take you for life."

"And will you reward me accordingly?"

"I promise nothing before hand"

—"Yes, this by way of earnest," cried I, catching her in my arms, and kissing her We were called to the other window, by an exclamation of Laurette's. "O, this is too much! support me, heaven! this is too much!"—She would have fallen to the ground, had I not flown to her, and supported her in my arms I bore her hastily to the garden for some air.

She was totally insensible Her head reclined on my bosom, with her face joined to mine. Emotions, to which I was before a stranger, that moment seized me I preſſed my lips to her pale cheek

We continued not long in this tender ſituation ſhe opened her eyes, and fixing them on me, conſcious,—tho' ſhe but hardly returned to ſenſe, of my gentle preſſures, "Save, O ſave me!" ſhe faintly cried "Leave me, leave me, Sir, to my fate"

"I cannot leave you thus, my adorable Laurnette Ah! do not command me from you"

"Ah! what is the meaning of this?" cried St Hermoire. "Ah! Laurnette, what are we to think?"

"Reproach not the wretched," replied ſhe. "Death, I hope, ſoon will end your enquiries, and my miſery" Again ſhe fainted She was now conveyed to her chamber, and put to bed

My ſpirits, by the late adventure, were ſo confuſed, I hardly knew what I did. I wandered into the garden, penſive and thoughtful

The ſweetneſs of manners I had diſcovered in Laurnette, on my firſt acquaintance, had given riſe to an eſteem, tender and ſincere. The ſudden change in her conduct, gave me infinite concern I beſought her once to tell me, in what I had been ſo unhappy as to offend her. "She warned me not to have ſo flattering an opinion of myſelf, as to imagine any behavior of mine, was of conſequence enough to bias her conduct" Such haughtineſs was not natural to her But her exclamation, her fainting, what appeared to be the occaſion of it, and a thouſand things which then occurred to my mind, raiſed a belief in me, that another ſentiment than hate, was the cauſe of the change I had experienced

The diſcovery filled me with complacency towards her I knew how to pity in her, the diſtreſſes I had experienced

I readily forgave her all the inquietudes ſhe had occaſioned

occasioned me, but I thought, and sighed at the thought, my pity was all I could bestow.

St Hermoine told me, Lauriette would not accept of any services from her, but repeatedly besought her to leave the room

She, in a faint voice, asked for her mother Madame de Montier came to her "What would my child have? What would my Lauriette?" "O, madam," she answered, "I have been very troublesome to you, but, I hope, I shall be no longer so Cousin, you leave us to-morrow,—perhaps, I shall see you no more—I cannot wish my days prolonged—May you, St Hermoine, be happy I need not pray for it!—you must be so."

"Ah! my Lauriette," she replied, "can I be happy, and see you thus? You bade me leave you. I am no longer dear to my cousin——What have I done to merit your hatred?"

"Reproach me not, my Adelaide, I have been long unhappy!"

"Why was my dearest child unhappy?"

"Oh! madam, my head, my heart, my soul was changed But I shall soon now be at rest in the assurance that I shall, very very soon, be no more, is my only comfort"

"What," said St Hermoine, to me, "are we to think? Love, it is plain, is her malady, and the object, admits not of a doubt"

"I said, "I looked on myself as highly indebted to Mademoiselle St Hermoine, for the intelligence she had given me, and that had I had the least suspicion of my not being disagreeable to the lovely Lauriette, I certainly should not have suffered so much, from her supposed cruelty But that my situation was an extremely delicate one, since were I now to make an offer of my heart to her acceptance, she might, perhaps, imagine it rather an act of compassion, than, as it would really be, the dvotion of a tender eſteem Were ſhe to recover her health, I would take the earlieſt opportunity of making propoſals to her father · and the ſecret, which St. Hermoine had honored me with, ſhould ever remain buried in my boſom "

I ſpent the night in anguiſh, a thouſand tormenting ideas, by turns, rent my heart I told St Hermoine, I would make propoſals to the family, yet my heart whiſpered me, it would not be thus diſpoſed of I had once taken the reſolution of perpetual celibacy, I could not change that reſolution, without the utmoſt pain When I reflected on the fate of Lauriette, her young and innocent breaſt wounded by hopeleſs love, I truly pitied her . ſo I ſhould have done, had I not been the object but I found my compaſſion roſe in proportion, as the ſufferings of my own heart, on a ſimilar occaſion, preſſed on my tortured memory What tears I ſhed ! What groans of anguiſh rent my burſting boſom

A dangerous fever ſeized Miſs de Montier —The phyſicians gave no hopes, her mother was in a ſtate of diſtraction

She thanked me for the tenderneſs of my enquiries after her daughter —" You know not, madam," said I, " the extreme intereſt I have in her recovery Could you ſee my heart, you would ſee how much of my future happineſs depends on it. Oh ! madam, let I hope you will in ſome happy hour become my advocate ! That I ſhall find in you, and monſieur, no obſtacle to my tenderneſs, for your amiable daughter "—" My ſon ! my dear ſon, let me call you, and I ſhall be bleſt "

" Ah ! madam ! will the dear Lauriette be ſaved "

" Oh ! this will make her well I wiſh not to conceal any thing from you I, in vain, endeavored to find out the reaſon of the change in Lauriette, yet could never find out the right one, till the

the evening she fainted; it then occurred to me, and I rather wonder it did not before, seeing how amiable you are, that my child had conceived a passion for you I communicated my suspicions to Minette, my maid, who brought up Lauriette, and loves her with a tenderness equalling my own. I thought to this faithful servant, she would be less reserved, than to any of her own family · I therefore appointed her to watch her, and by every artifice worm herself into her confidence. Now I knew she would not communicate any thing to Minette, but under the seal of secrecy, I determined to be apprized of my daughter's secret inclinations, concealed myself in a closet adjoining the bed, from whence a word could not escape me I did it, I hope, from a laudable motive, being unwilling to make Minette guilty of a breach of trust, as either way she must otherwise have been"

"Minette, after long professions of her love and services, told her, she wished she was worthy to be trusted with the secret, which, she was assured, was the cause of her malady. My daughter made no answer, but continued sighing.—At last, she said, in a low voice, "is my cousin gone? "Can you think they would go while you are ill?" I asked about my cousin, Minette, and you, say they ' 'Why, did not you mean to ask about Mr Mordaunt? Shall you not be sorry to part with them?' 'I do not know whether I ought ——And yet I always loved my cousin'—'And you do not hate Mr Mordaunt?—'What do you mean, Minette? —You are not so kind as you used to be.—Every body is altered, I think,—or rather is not the alteration in myself?—Ah! too truly it is. O, Minette! my once kind Minette, you ought to pity me!' 'Let these tears witness for me, how much I do pity you. Why will you not trust your faithful Minette.' 'O! my dear Minette, do not weep, I cannot bear to see any one in grief for me. I am not worth any one's tears.——I, that thought my self once so happy, but that is all over now.' 'Will my dearest young Lady forgive her servant, her friend?—I think I know your disease. Mitigate your grief by pouring part into my faithful bosom. Never shall it transpire; no one but me has the least suspicion.' 'Suspicion! of what?' almost breathless. 'Ah! Minette, hide me, save me from myself—I cannot bear my own reflections. Oh! you see into my inmost soul. You see my weakness—you see my passion,' said she, in a low whisper. 'Yes, Minette, I have yielded to a shameful passion for a man, who will despise me. My cousin, my happy envied cousin, is only worthy of him.'

"Minette strove to comfort her.——'Ah!' said Laurette, 'all that can be alledged in my favor, is my struggles against this fatal inmate. I knew not it was love, till too late. Yet, then I did all I could, but was unequal to the task. I loved learning, he indulged my propensity—fatal indulgence! fatal propensity! I took pleasure in his conversation. The air of melancholy, with which he was often overspread, rivetted me to him. He made me in part his confidante. I then found it was not the English books that gave me pleasure too, it was the society of my amiable tutor. My first sigh was, when I learnt he was not happy. He left us, and I became acquainted with the situation of my heart. I soon reflected with the deepest anguish, that I had conceived a passion for a man, who must be insensible to me; his heart was engaged, before he knew me. I numbered the sighs he had breathed for his fair ingrate. Ah! what days and nights of despair I endured!—To conquer or die was my determination. What were my sufferings before I could oblige myself to treat him

with

with indifference, I thought by that method to acquire a habit of perfect indifference But Oh! who can describe my torments, when jealousy was annexed to my former pangs—I could not support it—Yes, Minette, I am convinced he loves St Hermoine—and I have nothing to do but to die"

"I immediately left my place of concealment—Ah! unhappy Lauriette! I exclaimed. Foolish inconsiderate girl!———

"You have betrayed me, Minette! cried out my daughter, and instantly fainted I reproached myself for being thus precipitate she came to herself, but has been in a constant delirium ever since. Heaven will, I hope, restore her to our prayers,—if she dies, I have been her murderer"

I was highly enraged at Madame de Montier's conduct, however, I stifled my resentment, as her sufferings seemed sufficient.

I will pass over, madam, several occurrences, to acquaint you, that the many lucid intervals of Lauriette's delirium gave us great hopes In one of them, Mrs Montier acquainted her with my concern for her illness, and the proposal I had made her father, with intreaties, that they would use all their influence with her, to favor me with her hand, as soon as she recovered.

After some painful conflicts between her love and her delicate apprehensions, lest commpassion should have been the primary cause of my offer, she consented to see me as her lover She was just able to be carried into her dressing-room, which, when invited, I entered, not without emotion. But, good God! how was I struck with her appearance! Once blooming—now pale—emaciated, tho' still lovely A faint blush stole upon her languid cheek, when she heard my name announced. She answered my compliment almost inarticulately Her hesitation, her distress—all conspired to heighten my my feelings I, who could withſtand the luſtre of her eye, animated with luxuriant health, was now inſlaved by thoſe eyes dimmed by grief and ſickneſs, and half cloſed Her lovely mouth half opened to facilitate her quick reſpirations, her hand ſupporting her reclining head, were ſo many added charms in my eyes the knowledge too, that I was firſt beloved, ſtrengthened my growing attachment

Every day I was admitted to the preſence of my Lauriette, and had the ſatisfaction of ſeeing her daily recover. I then felt not the leaſt compunction at the thoughts of marriage The ſweet diſpoſition of Lauriette, her returning vivacity, and the uncommon affection ſhewed me by the whole family, gave riſe to a ſentiment, which, if it was not happineſs, was nearly allied to it.

As ſoon as the health of Lauriette was perfect, we were married, by the ambaſſador's chaplain, and afterwards by a romiſh prieſt for form-ſake only, my new relations being inwardly proteſtants, but were outwardly conſtrained to conform to the cuſtoms of their country

On the firſt birth-day of my wife, I gave an entertainment of muſic and dancing Honore, our eldeſt ſiſter, had the good-fortune to gain the heart of a very amiable young nobleman, of a proteſtant family She, generous and frank, was above diſguiſing her ſentiments: She told him ſhe loved him, as ſoon as ſhe felt that paſſion for him No obſtacles remaining, it was ſettled that they ſhould be married after my wife had recovered from her lying-in, which was then ſoon expected The little infant died in a few weeks, its death ſettled a melancholy on my Lauriette's mind, inſomuch as ſhe wiſhed to decline aſſiſting at the nuptials of Honore In hopes to amuſe her, we intreated her to be preſent, ſhe, in an evil hour, yielded to our perſuaſions.

When engaged in the joy of the day, her usual vivacity took place, she would dance After going down two or three country-dances, of which she was always fond, as being English, she complained of great thirst Ever attentive to her slightest wish, I went to procure her something warm, but in the interim she drank of the first thing she met with

I tenderly blamed her for not taking more care, "Don't say any thing," said she, "I may repent it" And clapping her hand to her forehead, said she was in violent pain, and begged to be carried out in the air I hastily led her into the next room, which opened by folding-doors into the garden She leaned on my arms —"Oh! my head, my head!" she exclaimed "Dear Mordaunt, I am very ill!" All assistance was procured, but too late, for that very instant the dear creature expired in my arms

Happily, for me, a state of insensibility prevented me from experiencing the poignancy of my affection at first The day which was ushered in with joyful festivity was concluded with lamentations

Every object at Tholouse served to remind me of my loss, my appearance there contributed to keep their wounds open It seemed our mutual interest to separate 'till time had mellowed our grief into a less painful reflection

I, a second time, yielded to the solicitations of De Montier, and accompanied him to Paris, whither he was going to prosecute an affair of the heart, with a young Lady he has since married

One day I met a man in the streets of Paris, whose face I thought no stranger to me, tho' I could not recollect where I had seen him However, I was impelled to speak to him, which I did in French, he answered me in broken accents I then told him in English, that I had seen him before.

He

He looked earnestly at me, then exclaimed, "good God! are you not Mr Mordaunt, Sir?" I assured him that was my name. "Then," said he, "you may know me possibly, Sir; I lived with Captain Archer." Do you live with him now? "No, Sir. I left his service about a year since, and am now come over to France with my present master."

"This is not a place, my friend, to converse freely; will you attend me into a hotel? I want to ask you many questions." We went into the first we came to. I could not resist the strong desire I had, of asking after you, madam. I enquired concerning your health, and whether you lived happy with the Captain, as I had not the least doubt, madam, that you were not married to my happy rival. "O, Sir," said he, "my late master, Cap. Archer, is not married. He continued to visit but a very little time at Vere-Park. And Kitty, Miss Vere's maid, told me her young Lady said, that whether what she had heard of your honor, and my master, was falsely or truely represented, she could pay your memory no less a compliment, than declaring she would never encourage the addresses of the Captain. My master was like a distracted man, when he was dismissed from Vere-Park."

"Miss Vere has since had several offers, but has rejected them all."

I thanked Robert for the intelligence he had given me, and having gratified him for his trouble, I went to my lodgings with emotions I thought long since extinct.

I was rejoiced to hear you were not married to Captain Archer. Being convinced he could not make you a good husband. I cannot say I was happy, because I felt all that tumult of doubts and anxieties which had so long rendered my existence painful: but I instantly relinquished my scheme of ending my days in a foreign land. I wrote to my cousin Lady Betty, and had the pleasure of receiving an answer full of tender reproaches. She informed me of her happiness, and conjured me to come and be witness of it. She told me—Ah! I must not repeat what she told me.—In the first moments of our interview, I had the misfortune to displease you.——Lord Charles C—— has intreated me to become his advocate.—Ah! madam, can I hope to succeed?

Excuse this melancholy recital, I, who cannot give pleasure, have no right to give pain.

Adieu, madam,

CHARLES MORDAUNT.

LETTER LXXXVII.

To Miss VERE.

May 9.

AH! Sidney! Sir John Evelin is arrived—O, my trembling heart, that it could beat itself to rest! Harriot is, in vain, striving to keep up some little spirit in me. Ah! I sink under these accumulating evils.

What means this? A post-chaise and four—the Evelin livery. And empty. Good heavens! a note!——An accident prevents his waiting on me. Lady Evelin begs I will make no delay, but come instantly to her. The future happiness, or misery of her family, depend on my speedy compliance. —Bids me haste, if I wish to find a mother.—Desires Mrs. Johnson may come with me.——A mother! O, gracious God! what accident is this? It

It is to Colnbroke I am to go——Ah! my beloved Sidney, pity your poor Caroline——I shall have no pretensions, when next I write, to the name of Melmoth; alas! had I ever any?

To that fatal indulgence, perhaps, I owe all my misery.

Continued by Miss DARNLEY.

Colnbroke.

Permit me, madam, to address you by the desire of our charming, yet unhappy friend. She is incapable at present. Yet be not too much alarmed; but prepare yourself to hear very strange, and unexpected events!

I accompanied Caroline and Mrs Johnson hither. The servant informed us, Sir John Evelin, on his arrival in England, took the first opportunity of waiting on a nobleman in power, in behalf of a very unfortunate person. He went on horseback, and was, as the servant thinks, very deep in thought, and regardless of his way, the reins laying loose, the horse fell with him, throwing him over his head, he was stunned with his fall, but they hoped there would be no ill consequence. Lady Evelin was coming to town to meet her son, and was time enough to be serviceable to him————

The dear Caroline exclaimed at the relation of the servant, clapping her hands, "when, O! when will my sorrows have an end! He was coming to me, when he met this fatal accident. Every one who concerns themselves with me, are marked out for sorrow.

When

When we arrived at the houſe, an elderly woman preſented herſelf at the chaiſe door; ſhe had the appearance of one who had been weeping.—— "Where, O! where," cried Caroline, "is Sir John? ſhew me inſtantly to him" The woman of the houſe begged ſhe would reſt herſelf a while in the parlour Mrs Johnſon fixed her eyes on her, and ſaid; "Sure I know your face" "You are not deceived," returned ſhe "You have often ſeen me, tho' I am much altered, as it is above twenty years ſince" "Still," ſaid Mrs Johnſon, "I cannot recollect you"——"You ſoon will. But pray inform me, which of theſe is the young Lady you received an infant from me."

"Good God! you are the very perſon Here," taking the hand of Caroline, "is the ſweet amiable"—"It is, it is,—I am ſure it is my child," cried out a lady, ruſhing into the room, whom I knew to be lady Evelin, and throwing her arms round the pale and trembling Caroline "Oh! every feature beſpeaks my long loſt daughter" "Daughter!" the dear girl repeated "Heavens! is it poſſible I have found a mother"

"O, yes! yes!" replied the lady, "Heaven has at length given you to my arms. Oh! 'tis too, too much! This extaſy!——But theſe tears will eaſe my throbing heart"

Caroline threw herſelf at her mother's feet, and in the moſt graceful and pathetic manner, implored her bleſſing. "O! my honored parent, bleſs your child, who, from this happy moment, will ceaſe to repine at the ills ſhe has ſuffered The privation of a mother' bleſſing, perhaps, has been the ſource of all——But how has this wondrous tale been unfolded"

"Another time, my lovely child, I will ſatisfy you, but, at preſent, my heart is ſo full of thee, —I loſe the remembrance of every thing elſe"

What

What a tender ſcene diſplayed itſelf I have not done it juſtice They both ſeemed regardleſs of every object, but each other the fond mother finding out freſh beauties in her lovely daughter — "Dear Angel!" ſaid ſhe, "The expreſs image of my beloved Sir John At that name Caroline ſtarted, and turned pale, lifting up her ſnowy hands, and fine eyes, to heaven "Ah! my God, what will become of him? Then ſhuddering,——My brother! Horrid, dreadful thought!"

"Ah! my poor ſon! Heaven will, I hope, ſoon reſtore him to health, time only can effect the reſt How ought we to adore the unſearchable ways of providence but for this accident, I ſhould not have known I had a daughter"

——"Ah! ſay no more," interrupted Caroline "How evident is the interpoſition of the almighty Ah! can I bear the dreadful idea? O, madam," running into her mother's arms, "Save me"

Her mother, kiſſing her cheek, was ſaying ſome kind conſolating things to her, when a ſervant entered. "My maſter is awake, and ſenſible. He inceſſantly calls for Miſs Melmoth He underſtands ſhe is here, and begs to ſee her"

"Ah! I cannot go —Do not, deareſt madam, inſiſt on it For heaven's ſake do you, in as gentle a manner as poſſible, inform him I cannot at preſent ſee him —Not till he can receive me as his ſiſter" We joined in perſuading the dear girl, that in his ſituation, he required ſoothing,—at laſt, we prevailed on her to go. I have been writing this ſince

What a complicated ſcene of diſtreſs, has this lovely Caroline been involved in I cannot forgive myſelf the ſmall and innocent ſhare I had in them But we were all ſtrangely infatuated and bewitched, by the diabolical artifices of thoſe abandoned wretches I hope ſome of them will meet their due re-

ward

ward in this life. I own this does not appear to me an uncharitable wiſh. I have no notion that we are to ſet ourſelves down contented with the misfortunes brought on us by the atrocious wickedneſs of others, and p[illegible]y with them all happineſs. I would forgive them, as I dare ſay Caroline will, with all her heart, but to ſay I would not, were it in my power, make any difference in the diſtribution of favors between them, and thoſe who had proved themſelves my friends——would, in my opinion, be very unjuſt to the worthy part of mankind. It would be ſurely incouraging vice and injuring—— Heavens! what is the matter?—They ſeem all in confuſion.——Great God! Caroline fainting, did you ſay?

Excuſe me, Miſs Vere.—I fly to my lovely friend.

Miſs MELMOTH in continuation.

The wretched ſport of fortune again takes the pen.

In what words ſhall I deſcribe to my dear Sidney, the cauſe of the confuſion which occaſioned Miſs Darnley to break off?

Trembling—and more dead than alive I gained the chamber of the unhappy Evelin.—O Sidney! I am deſtined to be the murderer of my brother! deprive a reſpectable parent of an only ſon!

My burſting heart and ſtreaming eyes, ſcarce leave me capable of giving you the dreadful relation.

As I entered the room, I heard the deareſt of men exclaim in a feeble voice; " will ſhe not come?

come? Will not my destined bride look on me, Evelin?" Think, what was my situation. I approached the bed, and gently putting back the curtain presented myself to him. His eyes sparkled with joy when he beheld me.

"This is kind—This is like my beloved Caroline. Ah! may I live to repay this tenderness!" I was weeping. "Do not weep," added he, putting out his hand, "and yet, those dear testimonies of your affection give me the sincerest joy. Sit down my life." I obeyed him. I held his hand in mine. "When we parted, my dearest Caroline, I little thought we should thus meet: but the assurance your last letter gave me, and the kindness of this visit, will soon enable me to fulfil my engagements. My mother too by her concurrence will render us happy."

"Compose yourself, my dear Sir John."—"You t[illegible] too much. You will retard the recovery so much wished by all your friends!"

"Only then give me the satisfaction of hearing you ratify the kind promises your letter contained—You are silent. Ah! Caroline, are you changed in so short a time?"

"My sentiments for you will admit no alteration. My esteem—my gratitude know no bounds,—they increase every moment."

"Esteem! and gratitude! It is your heart my lovely Caroline. Did you deceive me then when you vowed, seriously vowed you would be for ever mine? Cruel—cruel Caroline!"—The tears started in his eyes. I could not support the affecting sight, but throwing myself on my knees by the bedside, took his hand and bathing it with my tears, "call me not cruel, my amiable Evelin. Behold I am ready to do as you would have me. nay, to fulfil every engagement, if, when you are quite recovered, you should still think me worthy."

"And

"And wherefore ſhould I alter? If my return to health could poſſibly occaſion a change, I wiſh to die this moment Yes, my adorable Caroline, the hopes of ſpeedily calling you mine is the only cordial I can receive —But pardon my doubts.—Why will you not give me the ſupreme happineſs of hearing you expreſs a like impatience?"

"Believe me, the deſire to ſee you happy is the only wiſh next my heart —But ſo wayward has my fortune ever been, I am afraid to give way to the proſpect of happineſs, leſt ſome unforeſeen cloud ſhould intervene, and precipitate me into further miſery"

"We muſt not expect perfect happineſs we all know, but ſurely there will in our union be more than a bare chance for human felicity"

"Will my dear Sir John ſuffer me to plead his preſent indiſpoſition as an excuſe for my wiſhing him not at preſent to dwell on this ſubject? I am apprehenſive you are too much fatigued" He fixed his eyes on me ſtedfaſtly, without ſpeaking —After a long pauſe. "I have all along diſcovered an ambiguity in your words, which, from the known ſincerity of my Caroline, I cannot account for There is certainly ſome myſtery.—O tell me! eaſe my doubts or inſtant madneſs —Why thoſe tears? why this cautiouſneſs in you? why, when I urge you to make me happy, by an avowal of your affection, this backwardneſs? all theſe circumſtances concur to my belief of there being ſomething dreadful to be explained Ah! Caroline, can you thus ſport with the miſery of a man whoſe only wiſh is to make you happy."

"Witneſs for me heaven! cried I, weeping ſtill more, "with what injuſtice you accuſe me. Do I not now, by my ſolicitude for your recovery, evince my affection and tenderneſs for you?"

"While

"While the mind is on the rack, the body can feel no ease, tho' on a bed of down — Convince me," continued he, pressing my hand between both his, convince me there is no abatement in your affection"

"How shall I convince you?

"By vowing I shall possess this dear hand as soon as my illness has left me"—O, Sidney, how could I answer to this Would not compliance have been criminal in me, and a flattering his unhappy attachment? I answered with too much precipitation "Ah! do not urge me at present! —To-morrow—I will"——

"What will you do to-morrow?" he eagerly asked

"To-morrow I will give you my reasons" My excessive agitations alarmed him more than my words

Tell me, tell me what you mean?—Already my fore-boding heart whispers something dreadful —Keep me not, I conjure you in suspence.—Your guarded expressions sufficiently testify —A fresh flood of tears, which I could not restrain, made him more urgent—I continued. "The uncertainty of my birth makes me fearful of forming any connection My parents, you know, were strangers to me. The reflection of whose child I am is a lasting torment to me:—And I have lately learned you lost a sister"——

"Enough! it is enough Too well I know what you would say Great God! to all else I could submit" His agonies—agonies which my ill-fated precipitation brought on, threw him into a violent fit of coughing, he cast up great quantities of blood I shrieked out for help, and soon stood in need of it myself They carried me out of the room Ah! what did not my dear mother feel! I am amazed I keep my senses Is it just—but pardon

don me, merciful father, nor suffer me to add to my weight of guilt.

O! with what rapture I should embrace my parent!—But can she receive to her arms the murderer of her son?

I find the surgeons apprehend a vessel is broke by the fall.—O, good God! I have then been the cause of its bursting out afresh.—

May 10.

The dear Evelin is rather more composed. My poor mother strives all in her power to console him. He owned the force of her reasonings, and acknowledged his deep sense of her tenderness; but continually exclaims, "All else I could have borne! —But to have the crime of loving my sister too well, joined to the agonies I feel, is more than the human frame can support. My only wish is, by my death, to put an end to a passion interwoven with my existence." He then lies quiet, seemingly attentive to the consolatory arguments of his mother, but frequently sighs and lifts up his hand, while the silent tear strays down his pale grief-worn cheek.

Ah! why am I denied attending and watching over him? But I must check my inclination, lest I augment the pain of my too-unhappy brother.

My mother said she named me—"Ah! cease, dearest madam," he cried, "mention not that dear, too dear creature. Ah do not, I intreat you, by naming her, add to the guilt I am already overwhelmed with. Let me not hear her name.—I must, if possible—but I know it is in vain." Another time Lady Evelin begged him to compose himself, and take some rest. Do you think then, my dear mother, I am capable of rest? No.—that hope is over —" Do not say so, my beloved son," returned the weeping parent " Do my dear Evelin, for my sake, be still Don't talk any more, you will disorder your head " " You think then, Madam, I am not in my senses —Would to heaven I were not! that this was all illusion! but I too plainly feel I have all my senses, and am but too feelingly alive to all my woe " Lady Evelin knelt by the bedside, and put up fervent prayers to heaven for her beloved son —Ah! may they be heard! Gracious good God restore him to the prayers of a respectable parent, and the poor Caroline

Adieu —

May 11.

Thank heaven, my amiable brother is better —The physicians give us some little hope He seems composed,—has taken some rest, and is more resigned to his fortune He is a good man in every sense, that I hope will enable him to encounter and surmount his difficulties. How happy shall I be when he can behold me with the calm affection of a brother! How happy shall I be in such a parent! —such a brother!

It will, I fear, be some time before he can regulate his present unfortunate passion.

You will be, no doubt, impatient to hear the mystery of my birth cleared up My dear mother has seen many misfortunes Her days were a long time clouded Miss Darnley will give you the relation of these facts, partly from Lady Evelin's own mouth, and partly from a little transcript she lately made for her son's perusal.

My amiable brother pays me many flattering compliments. How new,—how delightful the praises

praiſes of a parent! Ah! I again repeat, when my dear brother is quite recovered, how infinitely bleſt I ſhall be!

I ſaid, when next I wrote, I ſhould have no pretenſions to the name of Melmoth. there is but one allay to the pleaſure I ſhould otherwiſe feel in ſubſcribing myſelf ever your

CAROLINE EVELIN.

LETTER LXXXVIII.

To Miſs Vere.

Colnbroke, May 12.

I Have taken ſome pains to tranſcribe Lady Evelin's hiſtory for the peruſal of dear Miſs Vere: it has coſt me many tears in the performance.

I know not whether you ever ſaw her Ladyſhip: her unfortunate ſon has all her features. She has been very handſome. I never beheld ſo lovely a mother and daughter as theſe; yet there is very little likeneſs between them, but a ſtriking one between Caroline and a miniature of the late Sir John's. "This," ſaid Lady Evelin, "was all I had to ſupport me through a ſea of troubles," "but now," throwing her arms round her daughter, "how am I repaid!"

The Hiſtory of Lady Evelin.

Sir Henry Evelin, father to my late beloved huſband, and the honorable James Hamilton my father, were brought up together. A childiſh attachment made them of the ſame party at ſchool, and increaſed with their years to the ſtricteſt friendſhip which continued unſhaken 'till they both married Their different connections made their interests different, though they ſtill kept up the friendly intercourſe, annually ſpending ſome time with each other

Sir Henry was, notwithſtanding, the reverſe of my father, he was haughty in his carriage—tenacious of his family and fortune, and above all piqued himſelf on *his father's* having a great ſhare in ſupporting the houſe of Hanover in its right of ſucceſſion *My father* was, unhappily of contrary principles He had ſtrongly imbibed the idea of the ſufferings of the S——t family it is therefore more to be wondered, that two men ſo oppoſite in their opinions ſhould ever be friends, than that the diſcovery of ſuch diſſimilarity ſhould make them enemies

Mr Evelin had confeſſed an attachment to me, I was fully ſenſible of his worth, and had juſt conſented he ſhould make propoſals to our reſpective families, when the fatal differences in the kingdom broke out, and almoſt every houſe was divided againſt itſelf My poor father ſided with the party he had ever ſecretly favored A breach between the families became inevitable Mr Evelin, certain he ſhould never now gain permiſſion to marry me yet unable to abandon me, preſſed me on his knees to accept him as my guardian and protector —My mother being dead, and my father engaged in ſo dangerous an enterprize We were both under age; but marriages at that time were not under the reſtrictions they now are He repreſented to me my ſad condition ſhould my father fall,—or the party, whoſe cauſe he eſpouſed, ſhould be cruſhed, as moſt likely it would be, at laſt, by dint of argument, and having a powerful advocate

in

in my breaſt, gained my conſent, and we were privately married

The event of the fatal undertaking is well known. After ſome engagements, wherein my father ſignalized himſelf, the party received a total overthrow —My unhappy, infatuated father fled, with many others, into France He was attainted, and all his eſtates confiſcated. He had a large ſum in the funds, but had drawn that out to help his leader

When I heard he was ſafe, I wrote to him, conveying my letter by a private hand, to acquaint him of my marriage, and to remit to him a ſmall ſum I had by me I could not have quitted England had he deſired it, being now very near lying in I lived very privately a few miles from London, under a feigned name, Mr Evelin viſiting me very ſeldom, but his tender behaviour and affectionate letters made me the happieſt of women, could I have been eaſy on my dear father's account

Mr Evelin was deſirous of attempting to gain his pardon, though ſuch a procedure would have endangered the diſcovery of our connection; but I was well aſſured, by a letter I received from him, that gaining a pardon would not inſure his ſafety, for he declared he was ſo well ſatisfied with the juſtice of the cauſe he had entered into, he would never quit it for any temporal advantage, and he ſhould, upon every occaſion, as much as in him lay, do all ſervice to the party he was determined to adhere to, as long as life and [illegible] remained This unhappy ſteadineſs in my father to a wrong cauſe, if we judge from conſequences, was the original ſource of all my misfortunes

Sir Henry (who had no ſuſpicion of his ſon's connection with me, though he had ſeen our mutual attachment) became deſirous of his marrying and told him what pleaſure it would give him to ſee him allied to a family he named, who were fervent in their attachment to the crown Mr Evelin gave vague answers to his father's hints, but when he spoke more plainly, he, with all submission, intreated his father not to bias his inclination. The young lady he allowed to have merit, but he thought himself yet too young to form a connection of that sort, which ought to be undertaken with great circumspection—Sir Henry, who was too proud to take the advice of any body, could but ill bear the being dictated to by a son, whom he looked on as his property, and answered with some warmth, "You did not think your youth an impediment, when you gave your heart to the daughter of that cursed traitor Hamilton Beware of your kindling suspicions in my breast, that you do not view that infamous race in the same detestable light I do Ha! you turn pale! Join with me, Evelin, unless you would have them mutiplied on your own head, join with me in cursing the execrable traitor and his family" His trembling son endeavoured to mollify his father's unnatural rage, by representing how unjust such a procedure would be, in the mildest terms But nothing could calm his passion At his feet my beloved husband fell, and implored him to believe better of him than to think he would act contrary to his duty in any instance but he could not—he dared not join in imprecating curses on a family already under the vengeance of heaven, no part of which had or were capable of offending him

Sir Henry told him, nothing could convince him he was not a rebel in his heart, but his immediate acquiescence to his proposal of the before-mentioned union Mr. Evelin begged to have some time to reconcile himself to so new a state; not from disinclination to the married life, but that he might gain a more perfect knowledge of the lady's disposition. Think what dreadful news this was for me?

I had

I had not seen my husband for above a week. I flew with open arms to receive him,—but started back on beholding the dejected air of his countenance; when he made me acquainted with the particulars, I burst into tears, and intreated him to forgive me the many distresses I had brought on him. Deplored my unhappy destiny that made me the instrument of his affliction. He clasped me fondly to his bosom, and uttered the kindest, tenderest assurances of lasting love. His presence, however, raised my spirits, and I again endeavored to render my humble dwelling appear pleasing to the best of men.

My dear little son, now growing engaging by its pretty ways, riveted our affection still closer. While my Evelin remained with me, all was joy; but when he left me, the cruel uncertainty of the reception he might meet from his father, made me most wretched. The only source from whence I could extract the least comfort, was the confidence I had in the faithful attachment of my dear husband.

By some means Sir Henry discovered what we had so long carefully concealed. It is easy for any one acquainted with his character, to conceive his rage and disappointment. He loaded Mr. Evelin with the most opprobious language, and imprecated the most horrid curses on us both: Curses which had but too fatal effect!

I was an utter stranger to these particulars, 'till I was informed in part by a billet I received from my husband, which contained only a few words, "that all was discovered, though he was ignorant by what means," adding, "nothing can equal my father's rage.—My mother, too, forgets the tenderness she once lavished on her son.—What the consequences will be I know not. I hope the cruel menaces I am threatened with are only a trial. Heaven preserve my dearest Caroline and her lovely infant!

No power shall make me relinquish my just claim to you,—you are my wife—I am convinced they cannot prove our marriage illegal."

What words can express my terrors and grief at the receipt of this? I read it over twenty times—Some of the expressions seemed so guarded, as left room for the most wounding doubts. But all my doubts and fears were soon realized. I was sitting weeping and caressing my child by turns, when the door of my apartment opened, and Sir Henry Evelin entered. I arose and shrieking out ran to the door involuntarily, as if I could avoid him.—"Do not fly me," said he, in a commanding tone, "I am come to make you an offer too generous for the invidious betrayer of a nation, and the daughter of a traitor."

I was almost sinking into the earth, nay, I should have esteemed it an happiness had it opened to receive me. Trembling, I fell at his feet, and lifted up my clasped hands to him, unable to articulate a sentence. "I repeat," continued he, nothing moved, I come to render you service, and will, if you comply with my request, be as much your friend as it is possible I can be to a rebel. I have authentic proofs of your secret correspondence with a traitor——a betrayer of his king and country. Your life, and that of your infamous parent are now in my hands. If you wish to save both from an ignominious death, renounce all claim to the wretch you have drawn from his duty, and I will suppress these papers in my hand——Speak, you know the alternative, chuse which you please."

"Life," said I, rising, "upon your terms I despise. What, give up my fair character to infamy? stigmatize my child? No, Sir, I am your son's wife, his lawful wife. Never will I be prevailed on to relinquish the right the law has given me."

"You

" You had better be advifed," faid he, with a menacing air

" Never, no, never will I take fuch execrable counfel, so help me, God !"

" There are ways and means of forcing you to terms —But I ftill hope you have fenfe enough to comply what is calculated for your intereft I fhall leave you a little time to confider my propofal "

" I require no time You have heard my final determination If my life is forfeited I fhall not repine at the injuftice of fuch proceedings But never will I voluntarily give up my name to lafting infamy I am, I repeat, the lawful wife of your fon, he knows I am, he could not agree to the horrid propofal you have offered me I glory in the title of his *wife* —I can give indubitable proofs that we were legally married Never will I, by denying it, give my children caufe [I was then with child] to curfe their mother "

" You are refolved then not to make me your friend ?"

" I abhor! I abjure your friendfhip You have ufed me too ill to lay claim to the refpect I wifh to feel for the father of my hufband "

" Hufband! Abandoned wretch! I will never believe my fon fo degenerate No, he impofed on you Come, I know he did —He was too wife to leave any proofs in your hands by which you could make any legal claim "

" I will not hear the beft of men thus afperfed. Know, to your utter confufion, I have the certificate of my marriage figned and properly witneffed "

" If I thought you were really his wife, I know not what I fhould fay to it To be fure he is ftill my fon — Will you, madam, permit me to look at your certificate ?" I confented, not fufpecting it in the heart of man to meditate the mifchief he defigned: For the inftant I took it out of a bureau, he snatched it from me, and tore it into a thousand pieces, asking me, with the most malignant smile, "if I had any other proof remaining?"

"There wanted not this proof," cried I, with indignation, "to convince me you are the most infernal monster breathing; but my claim is still the same, and shall for ever remain. Nor shall your menaces have any other effect than to heighten the contempt and aversion I already feel for you."

"'Tis well, madam; but you shall soon repent this insolent carriage. Soon will you be humbled." He went to the door, saying, "Gentlemen, walk in and do your office." Three ill-looking fellows came in, followed by the person to whom I had intrusted the letters to my called father. My poor little boy, terrified at the appearance of these wretches, clung to my neck, and cried out to me to save him. I clasped him to my bosom, telling him, for his sake, I would dare the worst.

Sir Henry advanced to me with looks of malice and rage. "You can no longer avail yourself of the alternative I before offered you. I consign you to these gentlemen, who are officers of justice."

"I know of no crime I have committed," said I, with all the fortitude I could assume. "I have therefore nothing to fear."

"Can you deny," said one of the horrid men, "your secretly corresponding with a declared enemy?"

"First tell me by what authority you dare thus to interrogate me?"

"I am a commissioned officer, madam,—a messenger. And give me leave to tell you, madam, a proper submission would be infinitely more becoming to you in your unhappy circumstances, than the haughtiness you have pleased to assume."

"You say true. My circumstances are very unhappy, indeed! I will endeavor to profit by your advice

advice But tell me to what purpose you have invaded my dwelling?"

"In a few words, madam, you must go along with us,—or relinquish your claim," said Sir Henry; "then will I suppress the evidence of that man in whose breath lies the life of your father"

"Ah! do not urge me to what I will never comply with." Come, come, madam," cried another, "you had better submit I wonder at Sir Henry's patience."

"I should not thus long have condescended to parly with you, had not Lady Mary F refused to marry my son 'till this affair was settled Yet once more, I ask you to sign your name,—your maiden-name, to this paper." I dashed it from me. "Urge me no more You know my resolution, and do your worst" But, O my God! what was the consequence? Even at this distant period my tears stream afresh —My heart still bleeds at every vein Nor can I yet reflect without horror upon the dreadful scene which was the result of my refusing to stigmatize myself and children with infamy!

"Since your child is your plea," said the monster, Sir Henry, "that shall no longer be so Tear him from her arms I have, by her own confession, some claim to him, and I will use it to prevent her ever seeing him again"

"You cannot,—you cannot, inhuman as you are, you cannot mean to deprive me of my only comfort! O take my life, but spare my infant" My haughtiness forsook me I threw myself on my knees before them, addressing, by turns, in the most supplicating distress One of the horrid wretches seized my screaming child —The three others held me All their united force could hardly restrain me I struggled, shrieked, intreated, all in vain.—The man who first took the dear infant, conveyed

conveyed him from my ſight. Ah! who can expreſs my feelings? The feelings of a tender mother deprived of her offspring! I exclaimed in the bitter eſt terms againſt the barbarity of Sir Henry. I was almoſt frantic. I tore my cloaths, and threw myſelf on the ground, bewailing my hard deſtiny in fruitleſs tears; the next moment ſcreaming for my darling boy——My voice became hoarſe. The deſcription of Hecuba, which I never read without freſh ſorrows, ſeemed a true picture of my affliction.

The baſe inhuman father of my huſband ſeemed to exult in my unheard of woe. I ſtarted up on my feet, the men each ſeized a hand, leſt I ſhould eſcape; they reſtrained my actions, but ſpeech was left me. "We yet ſhall meet, thou infernal monſter. I yet ſhall behold my lovely child and much injured huſband, when it will not be in thy power to blaſt our happineſs. Yes, in heaven we ſhall meet, where thou can'ſt never come." Thus I impotently raved, 'till my little remaining ſtrength was quite exhauſted, and I ſunk into a ſtupid inſenſibility. In which ſtate I was dragged into a coach, accompanied by the three men. I know not how far we went, but we ſtopped at a large houſe. I made no oppoſition when they told me I was to be confined there. I knew not what I expected, nor ſhould I, I believe, have ſhewed the leaſt ſurprize at any thing. A woman conducted me into a room ſtrongly ſecured by bolts, and bars at the windows; I did not make that obſervation then. I aſked no queſtions, but gave myſelf entirely up. Every idea ſeemed loſt. I threw myſelf on a bed, and I remember no more of any occurrence for ſome weeks. At the end of that time, I found myſelf very weak and reduced: I ſuppoſed I had been ill, but had not curioſity enough to enquire what kind of indiſpoſition it was.

In

In a day or two my mental faculties began to strengthen, and then the remembrance of my sufferings returned, with all their bitterness Every hour they seemed to acquire new force. I spent my time in continued lamentation.

One morning, without any previous notice, the vile Sir Henry entered my room "Ah! what brings you hither?" cried I, all out of breath; "I have no more children to be murdered You will spare the infant I yet bear, because it is not sensible of injury"

"Your child is safe: Though henceforward it must be a stranger to you All I have now to acquaint you with, is, that Lady Mary F is now satisfied my son is under no binding engagement, but you will make us perfectly easy by signing this paper"

"If my consent is necessary, I will never give it. I know Mr Evelin can never marry while I am living. If he is desirous of entering into so solemn a connection with another, let him complete the work begun by you, let him plunge his sword in that heart already wounded in the tenderest part — Tell him, for him I wish to live—for him I would freely die · But I will never give sanction to so black a crime I cannot be guilty to my offspring. You know how much I can bear, how much I *have* borne in defence of my legal claim If he can thus cast me from him—which I will never believe—it is a still more forcible call on me to protect my own honor, and that of my children I have suffered, Sir, a great deal, how much, you, the cruel perpetrator, need not be told I have been unjustly confined, — My child torn from me —I have only your base word,—and how well I can depend on that I too fatally have seen, that he is safe, that the dear angel is yet living You see, Sir, I am now calm.——My griefs have divested me of that haugh-

haughtineſs of which you complained. I would, as it is my duty, and was ever my wiſh, obey my huſband in all things; but I ſhould become equally criminal with my perſecutors, could I join their impious endeavors to divide a union formed in the preſence of God."

"I ſee plainly," ſaid he, "mild meaſures will never do with you. I leave you to your own reflections."

I ſtill had ſo much confidence in the fidelity of my huſband, I did not give myſelf wholly to deſpair; but the thoughts what his ſufferings might be, wrung my heart.

About a fortnight after this converſation, a letter was brought me, it bore the hand-writing of my huſband, directed to Mrs Menil, the name we had aſſumed. I opened it trembling, as if I had afore knowledge of the ſoul-freezing contents.

In it he told me, "He had been married about a week. That his ſufferings had been great before he could come into ſuch meaſures; but that there was no other way to regain the affection of him, to whom he owed his being, and which he had forfeited by his unhappy connection with me. The child, he aſſured me, was well, but I muſt never hope to ſee it, leſt, for his ſake, I ſhould endeavor to renew my claim. He wiſhed me a happier lot than I had hitherto drawn; and intreated me never to attempt ſeeing him, as I muſt now be, if poſſible, forgotten by him."

It is impoſſible any one, unacquainted with ſimilar grief, to conceive what was then my diſtreſs. But in time my ſorrows a little abated; that is, they were not ſo outrageous as at firſt, but ſtill loſt not their poignancy.

I continued in this place a month longer, when one day the woman told me, Sir Henry had left me at liberty to go whither I pleaſed. "And whither ſhould

should I go?" asked I, weeping "I had a home,—I had a husband,—I had a child—All, all are torn from me,——whither should I go?"

Wherever you please Mr Evelin and his Lady are gone abroad for these two years—You may live where you will. Sir Henry will make you a reasonable allowance Here is a bill for one hundred pounds to begin with"

All places were now alike to me, yet I had a desire to change My former house I could not bear the thoughts of. I removed to a retired place, some miles distant In six weeks after my settling, I was delivered of a daughter Her birth was a fresh source of affliction to me I had brought a little innocent into the world to be miserable as myself I had given her wretchedness for her mother, but who was her father?

The cruelty and injustice of my husband weakened my strong attachment to him, but the birth of my daughter awakened all the mother, all the wife. For her sake I became more careful of my own life, and more resigned to my fate

Ah! what tears have I since shed on her account! I have always, without abandoning myself to imaginary ills, had sufficient sources of affliction.

I lived the most recluse life, never seeing any one but the woman with whom I lodged I never hinted the least to her of my circumstances

When my little Caroline was a year old, she was taken with the small-pox, which proved of the most favourable kind, a mother's anxiety filled me with a thousand fears—Those of my Landlady were scarcely inferior, so attached was she to the pretty innocent On the ninth day the small-pox were about the turn, when Mrs Lodge gave me a letter, brought by a strange man The direction was Mr Evelin's My emotions were a long time too strong to enable me to open it At last I gained resolution,

resolution, reflecting nothing could make me more wretched What was my astonishment at reading these words

" Ah! my ever adorable Caroline! if this comes not too late, if yet the heart of my beloved is not quite broken by the cruel treatment she has received, O pity! and lend an ear to the sorrowful complainings of your tender husband Yes, my Caroline! —whatever wicked suggestions have been infused into your mind, I would not forego that title to be master of the world

" I have just discovered the deep dissimulation which has been practised to render us both wretched Great God! I thought you were dead,—I have hitherto dragged a painful existence but if you will bless me with your presence, we yet may be happy Will you, my Caroline—my wife—— hasten to a husband, who has never ceased to adore you? A long illness which I have laboured under prevents my travelling—I can scarce hold my pen to give you these assurances of my tenderness and love. You may safely rely on the bearer of this. He is furnished with every thing to facilitate your journey to the arms of your faithful husband,

JOHN EVELIN"

I asked a thousand questions of the messenger He told me he had taken a passage for me in a vessel that was to sail in two days And, to prevent any suspicion on my side, as he knew forgeries had been used, he shewed me my own picture, which Mr Evelin had given him for that purpose, and which, being set in a particular manner, could leave no doubts

Eager to behold this dear husband, I hastily packed up my things My infant I could not think of taking with me, nor could I wait her recovery, the messenger telling me in how bad a way my beloved Evelin was What could I do? I, in an evil hour,

hour, confided my precious charge to the care of Mrs Lodge, leaving a sum of money with her for its maintenance, till I could send for it, which I purposed doing as soon as I was settled abroad

Harrison had a chaise ready for me, so kissing and blessing my dear little Caroline—Caresses which, alas! were never to be repeated, I took my leave of her and England

We had been but a few hours in the vessel before a most dreadful storm arose We were in incredible danger Our ship springing a leak, we were constrained to take to the boats. We had hardly crowded into them, when the vessel and whole cargo sunk to the bottom A report a long time prevailed that all the crew perished

The storm continued, with unabated fury, for eight and forty hours The horror of our situation is inconceivable, abandoned to the tempestuous ocean in a long-boat What added to our distress, was the sight of the other boat's crew perishing, ourselves unable to afford them the least assistance, and each moment expected to share their fate

In the morning of the third day we espied land; and, by the help of glasses, discovered it to be the Danish coast so far had we been driven without compass

We fortunately made land, where money procured us relief As soon as I had a little recovered my fatigues, I embarked along with Harrison a second time for Ostend, where we safely arrived. I made all haste to Bruges, where my Evelin was settled Ah! how tender was his reception of me Words cannot express the emotions of two persons meeting after so long, so cruel a separation, and each suffering as we had done Mr Evelin, after some time told me, it was owing to the person appointed for his governor, that he found out my dwelling. He repeated his sufferings, inflicted by his hard-hearted father,

father, to force him to comply with the disannulling our marriage

Sir Henry, when he found intreaties could not prevail, informed his son, he had proof of my secretly corresponding with the rebellious villain Hamilton, and, with all calmness, shewed my husband the letter I had, indeed, wrote one, and entrusted it to the care of one I thought could be confided in, but, I take heaven to witness, I never wrote to the least circumstance relative to political affairs, though such appeared, which had artfully been added to the end of my letter, the sight of which gave Mr Evelin the greatest apprehensions, judging that his father would willingly bring my life into danger, tho' his own family were involved in the same ruin Another accusation, was my sending supplies to the enemy It is true, I twice sent my exiled father a sum of money The last was a bill of a hundred pounds, which Mr Evelin presented me with on the birth of my son He asked me, laughing, "What I would do with it?" I answered, "his bounty to me made it unnecessary for me to keep it but that my poor father was in penury and want, while I was rich and happy I would therefore, with his permission, send it to him" There wanted not witnesses to prove the validity of these charges, should it be brought to a trial, which Mr Evelin was threatened with, unless he would comply with his father's schemes.

Some time afterwards he acquainted my husband I was taken into custody, and one of the jailers brought him a letter as from me "Wherein I lamented my not having it in my power to see him, &c that my last moment was approaching, which gave me the more concern, as I died disclaimed by him, for whom I fell a martyr"

He was led to believe I was dead A certificate of that and my burial being shewn him.

Lite

Life now became odious to him His father pretended great contrition for the part he had acted, but still pressed him to marry. this he strenuously refuled Sir Henry then advised him to go abroad, and appointed him a companion · Mr Evelin was too weak to hold many conferences with his inhuman parent, and therefore made no objection to the person, though he thought it was only exchanging one jailer for another He left England, making a solemn vow never to return to it while his father lived

They settled at no particular place, but continued travelling about Mr Evelin never conversing more than was just necessary with Mr Walton, whom he considered as an agent of Sir Henry's

Time, which generally weakens the greatest sorrows, seemed to add to Mr Evelin's melancholy. After long struggling with the worst of disorders, he was just sinking under it Mr Walton, who was a compassionate man, strove all in his power to gain the confidence of his pupil, and console him He urged him to take care of his health, and not to waste his life in repining for a worthless wretch, who was deservedly abandoned This brought on a warm answer from Mr Evelin, an eclaircissment was the consequence

Mr Evelin learnt, to his great joy, I was living, and Mr Walton was convinced he had been basely deceived by Sir Henry He acquainted my husband with the place of my residence in consequence of which we happily met again

I informed Mr Evelin of the birth of my daughter, and in what manner I had settled her As the winter was nearly approaching, we agreed to let her remain in England till it was past

The great fatigue, I had undergone, threw me into a fever, but time, and the tender assiduity of the best of men, soon restored me. As soon as I

was

was a little recovered, I wrote to Mrs. Lodge, as I had promised to inform her of my arrival, and in what manner I was settled she being wholly ignorant of each interesting event of my life Harrison, indeed, mentioned before her the name of the vessel and captain, with whom we were to sail The mail, by which I wrote, was unfortunately lost, which circumstance I knew not 'till some months after

I had a strong desire to see my dear father We wrote to him, but had the misfortune to hear he had been dead three months This was a great affliction to me; and, joined to my separation from my dear children, needed all the tenderness of Mr Evelin to enable me to support

In about a year, the birth of a son gave us each great joy. My attendance on him weaned me a little from the constant thoughts of the others, though I had all the mother in my heart for them, I yet ceased to lament their absence so bitterly The death of this dear little infant, when about eight months old, was so severe a blow to me, as I believe I could not have survived, had not my grief been drawn into another channel, I mean a dangerous illness which seized my husband In my apprehensions and tears for him, I forgot my child

Sir Henry's death, in a few months, recalled us to England With what rapture did I embrace my beloved long lost son But notwithstanding every inquiry, I never could hear of my lovely little daughter, ever remaining an absolute stranger to the fate of that helpless infant

I never knew another grief till the death of Mr Evelin, which happened about six years ago. and though blessed with the best of sons, I have never ceased to look forward to that heaven that contains my dear husband.

Thus

Thus ended Lady Evelin's transcript I shall remit to you the subsequent conversation with her ladyship, which will explain to you by what means she discovered Caroline to be her daughter

Sir John, notwithstanding the physicians flatter his mother, is in imminent danger, throwing up large quantities of blood on the least movement Poor Lady Evelin! poor Caroline! how does misfortune crowd on you!

I am, dear Madam,

Yours obediently,

HARRIOT DARNLEY.

LETTER LXXXIX.

To Miss VERE.

Colnbroke, May 13.

LADY Evelin received a letter from Sir John—which I believe has been before intimated—to request her presence in town She was coming up, when one of Sir John's servants met, and acquainted her with his accident. I speak in her own words.

Excessively alarmed at the intelligence I received, I hastened thither, where I was informed my son was carried I found him insensible The surgeons who attended him, gave great hopes, tho' they scrupled not to say he was inwardly hurt

The first return of reason he used to beg I would send to Miss Melmoth, as without her life, was not worth

worth preserving I assured him I would dispatch a servant for her the next morning, when I hoped I should be so happy as to see his choice He expressed his acknowledgments by his eyes and a gentle pressure of my hand. It was requisite for him to be left quiet, so I went down stairs into the parlor

I sent Harrison to beg to see the gentlewoman of the house, and was beginning to express my obligations to her, but she interrupted me by asking, if I was mother to Sir John Evelin? assuring her I was. "then" said she, "I am mistaken for when I first saw your ladyship I could have sworn I had once known you"

I then fixed my eyes on her, and said; "I too think—Nay, I am sure O my God! was not your name Lodge?"—"It was madam; and if I may credit my eyes you once was called Menil"

"O then for God's sake! where is my child? Why did you not answer my letters?" She told me a long story which sufficiently convinced me I should find my long-lost, long-regretted child in the person of Miss Melmoth She had heard the ship was cast away, and all the souls perished —The loss of the mail prevented her hearing from me.—She married, and changed her habitation —Her husband traded to Scotland he wanted her to go and settle with him. she consented, purposing to take the little Caroline with them, of whom they were equally fond That about this time the housekeeper of Mr. Melmoth used to take notice of the little prattler, and frequently had it at the castle. Mr. Melmoth became attached to it. and pressed Mrs Lodge to leave her with him. She told him all she knew of its history she knew from my melancholy I had been unhappy She likewise knew I went by a feigned name. She told him of my hastily quitting her house, and being lost at sea. In short, she

thought

thought she acted, as the parents of the child would have commended her for, by giving her such a protector. From Scotland she went to Holland, where she continued till within these two years Thus every circumstance concurred to keep us in ignorance of each other, had not the mercies of providence interposed

What were my agitations! tho' I had not a doubt of your being my child From the picture Sir John had drawn of you, I had great reason to believe you amiable! but how agreeably were my expectations augmented, by a sight of your person. I could not repel my inclination, but rushing into the room, clasped the loveliest of daughters to the bosom of the tenderest of mothers.

Indeed, Lady Evelin seems so inchanted with the sweet Caroline, that her apprehensions for her son give place to her joy The surgeon says, Sir John's accident from the first was attended with very dangerous symptoms These frequent discharges of blood must wear him out And his little attention to his own safety, has greatly contributed to make him worse.

The dear Caroline gives herself up to melancholy ideas, her mother endeavours to flatter herself that he will recover

Helpless, ill-fated Evelin! How little has he merited his sufferings!

This morning he said to Lady Evelin, "I observe, my dearest mother, with what industry you avoid mentioning a name you think would raise emotions in me, hard to be suppressed You conceive hopes of my recovery from my silence, and seeming resignation: but ah!" sighing, "it is in vain—It is here?" pointing to his heart "You ought not to wish me to live, since to lengthen my moments would but lengthen my despair and guilt.—I cannot repent I cannot cease to love the

the too amiable Caroline." Lady Evelin had just been telling me this. I sat weeping. Caroline entered. "Ah! my sweet friend in tears, if you weep, how should the wretched Caroline express her sorrows? Say, my Harriot, is there any fresh cause for grief? My mother—Ah! how sweet that word, were it not accompanied by so cruel a pang! My mother I find has but just left you. What said she of my beloved brother? Why am I not permitted to attend him? But I, unhappy cruel destiny, am doomed to be the cause of all. Ah Harriot! continued she, folding her arms round me, and mingling her tears with mine, "the vindictive imprecation of a cruel father is visited on his children.—The hand of heaven is against us. Here comfort," cried I weeping, "you may yet see happier days."

"Ah no!" was her reply.

She insisted, in so pathetic a manner, to hear what her mother had said to me, I could not resist. "I have never ceased to pray," said she, "for the recovery of my dear brother.—And does he wish to die?—Cut off in the bloom of life, and his hapless sister the cause of his death."

May 15.

What a scene have I been witness to! Never, no never will the sad traces be worn from my memory.—I know not how to write—and yet it is necessary to give vent to the overwhelming grief that fills my heart.

Lady Evelin was attending her son, who had yesterday begged to have a divine with him. This morning he said, "Will my mother, ever kind and indulgent, grant my wish? The only wish I now can form. I have, from the conversation of the worthy clergyman, and the knowledge of my own dissolution, brought my mind into a more proper state. My end is approaching.—Ah! madam,

let

let not that assurance augment your grief. I cannot support the idea of quitting life without taking an eternal leave of one I am authorized to love in some degree, and though I have exceeded the bounds prescribed of brotherly affection, I have a sincere hope, a crime, unknowingly committed, will be forgiven me. The pangs I have endured,—for sure they have been exquisite, but they will soon be over,—I trust will be received as an expiation. I am now perfectly resigned to my fate.—— Will you join your intreaties with my dying ones, to induce my —— ——sister to pay me one short visit."

Lady Evelin attempted to dissuade him. "I would not, my dear madam, have made this request, did I not know the emotions her presence may occasion will have little effect on my life. The surgeon this day confirmed my suspicions; and let me add my hopes, that a very little time and I shall cease to be wretched."

With tears of maternal anguish did Lady Evelin deliver the sad request of her dying son. I was writing, and Caroline came into the closet. "Ah! Harriet!" said the dear afflicted mourner, "I must see my unhappy brother.—It is his request. Good God! how shall I support the awful meeting!"

It was with great difficulty she assumed courage to enter his room. I was forced to accompany her. The bed curtains were undrawn for air. The pale, emaciated Evelin was raised in his bed, supported by his weeping mother, who continually applied eau-de-luce to prevent his fainting. "How kind!—how exquisitely kind!" murmured forth Sir John, the broken accents almost dying on his pallid lips. He held forth his hand, which Caroline taking, pressed it to her lips, unable to speak, and pale as ashes. A faint blush overspread his face, his eyes beamed a lustre, which, from one in his situation, one ſhould ſcarce think poſſible. Repeated ſighs burſt from his boſom; tears ſtood trembling in his eyes. Ah! my dear ſon," ſaid Lady Evelin, "I feared you would be too much harraſſed. Had we not better retire?"

"Oh, no, by no means.—I had flattered myſelf I could have borne this ſight without emotion. Ah! how frail is man! Yet leave me not. It is but a little time I requeſt your ſtay.—I wiſhed to ſee you," gazing on Caroline——"To tell you, I feel myſelf happier now than for ſome tedious days paſt. Four long tedious days have I paſſed ſince laſt I ſaw you. Yes, my Caroline! my ſiſter! great have been the agonies I have felt; but they will be ſoon over. The time, my beloved ſiſter, is at hand, when even your idea will loſe its faſcinating charms. I ever loved you, in my moſt indulgent hours of hope, with the purity of angels. Heaven, in compaſſion to my ſufferings, has ſanctified that love. I dare now avow it. No guilty thought now governs with impetuous ſway. Reaſon and Religion have their force. Yet think not I could thus philoſophize, did I not know my death inevitable. Ah! no, I feel, were I to live, I ſhould ſtill be criminal.—I could not tear the too-long indulged tenderneſs from my heart. By dying alone can I regain my peace; wiſh not therefore, my deareſt friends, for a prolongation of my life, ſince that would be only a protraction of miſery. O death! acceptable art thou to the needy, whoſe ſtrength faileth him, and is vexed with all things, to him who deſpaireth, and hath loſt all hope."

Caroline, with a freſh burſt of tears, eagerly preſſed his hand between her's; with great difficulty ſhe articulated theſe few words. "Ah! live, my amiable brother! my Evelin! I cannot bear to part with you. Ah! ſtrive to live, and time may reſtore you. Heaven may ſtrengthen your mind

—You

—You may be enabled to behold me, with the affection of a relation."

"Were I deſirous of life, I am convinced, that would be impoſſible. I am ſenſible there is now but a ſhort ſpace between me and eternity. That reflection muſt give us all a pauſe. O may my ſincere repentance of youthful follies meet acceptance! And may you, my beloved mother and ſiſter never know any other pain than the loſs of me! A few tears, my ever reſpectable parent, I will allow you to ſhed, for a ſon who never, ſince reaſon had power over his actions, willingly gave you offence. But turn your eyes there," looking at his ſiſter, "and receive conſolation. Think, that if death has deprived you of one child, you poſſeſs another, in whom every perfection is centered. Cheriſh her, for her own ſake; and though no farther inducement is neceſſary, for my ſake love her ſtill more. I have offended. I could not repent my offence—I die for it." He was too much fatigued and agitated to proceed farther. Lady Evelin and her unhappy daughter were in agonies. Good God! I have done great injuſtice to the awful ſcene, but I was myſelf too much affected to attend to circumſtances.

Dear Caroline! words are too weak to paint thy diſtreſs. Ah! had you ſeen her, her ſtreaming eyes turned up to heaven, her ſnowy hands claſped and lifted up, her trembling lips ſilently ſupplicating—your tears would have guſhed as mine did, and ſtill do. My eyes are become fountains.

Ah! all hope is vain. The ſurgeon bade them expect the worſt. Poor Lady Evelin! the dear Caroline drowned in tears, threw herſelf at her mother's feet. "O my mother! Can you forgive your child? But for me, perhaps—my unhappy, ill-fated brother,"—Sobs choaked her voice. Lady Evelin snatcht her from the ground, and pressed her to her bosom. I left them both in speechless agony, weeping in each other's arms.

I must go to the afflicted Caroline, yet, I cannot afford her the least comfort. I sit and weep with her, unable to say any thing capable of assuaging her grief. Ah! how vain is all the sophistry of argument against real evils!

May 17, Four-o'Clock.

It is all over, as the surgeon predicted; a fit of coughing seized the unfortunate Evelin, and he was suffocated.

Expect not particulars. O! may the distress of this wretched family end here! Lady Evelin! unhappy mother! Caroline! Dear creature!—— but I check my pen.

This life is not the scene of happiness. Virtue here meets not its reward.

I make no apologies, dear madam, for breaking off. You have shed tears enough, I question not. I am almost blinded by them. Ah! would to God I could alleviate the sorrow of the afflicted pair!

The dear Caroline this instant looked in upon me. "Tell my beloved Sidney," said she; then clapping one hand to her eyes, and with the other striking her breast—"I cannot speak," she hurried out of the room. I hear her weeping. Ah! may these friendly tears relieve her! Adieu! madam,

Yours,

HARRIOT DARNLEY.

LETTER XC

To Miss MELMOTH

Vere-Park, May 20

WEEP on, my amiable Caroline, let your tears freely flow Grief, which from circumstances will admit of no alleviation but time, should be left to itself Its own violence alone can afford the wished-for relief

The mind, weakened by continual sorrows, is apt to imagine every additional ill as the greatest The distresses which have been heaped on you, may naturally suggest that idea, but in the midst of your tears and lamentations, let the kind, consolatory thoughts recur to you, which you so tenderly, so efficaciously expressed to me on a similar occasion Let me repeat to you the little extract you made from a moral tale, well adapted to our mutual afflictions.

" Sorrows, said *Honadu*, O duteous *Urad*, which arise from sin, or evil actions, cannot be assuaged without contrition or amendment of life, with these, the soul is deservedly afflicted, and must feel before it can be cured Such sorrows may my amiable pupil never experience! But the afflictions of mortality are alike the portions of piety and iniquity It is necessary we should be taught to part with the desirable things of this life, by degrees, and that, by the frequency of such losses, our affections should be loosened from their earthly attachments

" While you continue to be good, be not dejected, O my obedient *Urad*, and remember, it is one part of virtue to bear with patience and resignation the unalterable decrees of heaven, not but that I eſteem your ſorrow, which ariſes from gratitude, duty, and affection, I do not teach my pupil to part with her deareſt friends without reluctance, or wiſh her to be unconcerned at the loſs of thoſe, who, by a marvellous love, have ſheltered her from all thoſe ſtorms which muſt in a moment have overwhelmed her helpleſs innocence. Only remember that your tears be the tears of reſignation, and that your ſighs confeſs an heart humbly yielding to his will, who ordereth all things according to his infinite knowledge and goodneſs*."

Could we expect our friends immortal? you ſaid. Could we wiſh it? How cruel, how ſelfiſh that wiſh! Do we not wiſh thoſe happy whom we love? How incomplete was their felicity in this world! O, my beloved Caroline! where could the virtues of my excellent mother and your amiable brother meet their reward, but from the Almighty, who has reſumed them to himſelf?

I muſt chide you, my lovely friend, if you ſo harſhly reflect on yourſelf as the cauſe of this melancholy event. If we look back to cauſes, we muſt go to periods before your exiſtence, even to the fatal anathema of a cruel and unjuſt father: Nay, I know not, if we might not go ſtill further; but we ſhould never have finiſhed our reſearches, if we endeavor to find out the whole concatenation of circumſtances that make our fate.

We are apt to look up to the happineſs of others, without looking down on their miſeries. After you have paid the tribute of tears and ſighs, let your reaſon and religion ſooth your ſoul. By time and theſe aids, I hope to ſee you reſtored to that peace which has too long been a ſtranger to your care-worn breaſt.

We have been a long time ſeparated, our meet-

* See the Tales of the Genii.

ing

ing is not far distant My father will give me permission to attend you at Evelin-Abbey, whither I learn, by Miss Darnley, you are soon to go

If Lady Evelin in the least resembles her lovely daughter, I doubt not in the least being welcome O my Caroline! I long to fold you to my heart,—that heart that bleeds for your sufferings—To weep with you, and share your griefs

Adieu, my best love,

SIDNEY VERE.

LETTER XCI.

To Lady BETTY CRAUFORD

Evelin-Abbey

AS your ladyship has so tenderly interested yourself in the fate of the little Sidney, she makes no apologies for giving you a correspondent, by which means you will become further acquainted with the story of my amiable Caroline

I know not how to describe our first interview, as my emotions, tho' infinitely short of my lovely friend's, were strong enough to deprive me of attention to any thing else

The dear Caroline rushed into my arms. O my Sidney! My Caroline! was all we could utter. The meeting of two friends has always something affecting in it, we used always to be melted but now, the recollection of all the distress she had suffered since our separation, bursting at once on her mind, was too powerful My tears forced themselves a passage, happily she caught the soft contagion, which most probably saved her from a fit: I interrupted her not, indeed I was not capable

After an hour spent with my Caroline, I was introduced to Lady Evelin· a most lovely woman indeed! As Miss Darnley says, Caroline has very

 little

little perſonal reſemblance to her: her unhappy ſon, had all the ſweetneſs of countenance, joined to a perfect maſculine figure. You my dear Lady Betty have ſeen him.

The huſband of Lady Evelin, by his portrait, muſt have been extremely handſome. Caroline has the moſt feminine likeneſs of him that can poſſibly be: ſhe has all his features ſoftened to the moſt harmonious delicacy imaginable. I have often thought her complexion alone would have given beauty to bad features, and her features, without the help of complexion, render'd her lovely.

An air of deep, and I think habitual dejection, was ſpread over the face of Lady Evelin. Her melancholy prevented not her polite and friendly reception of me.

" I have, every moment, more reaſon to be pleaſed with my Caroline," ſaid ſhe, " what can give me a higher idea of her underſtanding than the choice of her friends? I have the greateſt obligation to the amiable Miſs Vere: ſhe was a friend to my child in the moſt extenſive ſenſe, when all the world beſide forſook her."—But was I to repeat all the civil things ſhe ſaid, you would think I took pleaſure in reciting my own praiſe, which, however proceeded rather from the goodneſs of Lady Evelin's heart than my deſert.

" My daughter has given me a little detail of her paſt life, if ſhe has no objection, I ſhould be happy to ſee her letters, that I might know my full extent of happineſs in poſſeſſing ſuch a treaſure."

" O, my dear mother!" ſaid Caroline, I fear you will find many reaſons to retract your opinion, but yet you ſhall ſee them, for gentle will be the reproof of my honored parent."

Lady Evelin tenderly preſſed her to her maternal boſom. Then taking my hand and joining it to Caroline's, kiſſed each. " I will leave you, amia-

ble

ble friends, for a little while." She went, I believe, to give vent to a sorrow which I observed rising to her eyes.

I ran on in her praise, as well to divert Caroline's attention, as to give myself relief. With what transport did she listen to me! "O my dear Sidney!" said she, "What a mother! what a friend do I possess! But one, but one allay," added she, melting into tears. "But come, my love," she continued, drying her eyes, "I am strangely negligent: some refreshment must be necessary." She chearfully gave orders for chocolate, and we chatted agreeably on indifferent subjects, if I may use that expression, when your ladyship was part of our conversation.

This morning we rambled in the Park. Caroline observed to me it was a charming place, but said, she had not yet been capable of tasting its beauties. She repeated, in the softest accents, these lines of Milton.

With what delight could I have walk'd thee round,
If I could joy in aught, sweet interchange
Of hill and valley, river, woods and plains.

I took an opportunity from talking of Lady Wilton, to advert to Sir George. Caroline gently sighed. After a pause. "That is a subject I have not yet dared to trust myself with.——Reflections will recur, notwithstanding our efforts to the contrary. —I am neither insensible or ungrateful, I must therefore acknowledge Harriot's delicacy; she never once, since an unhappy event, has mentioned her brother's name. But, since we have, I must tell you my apprehensions on Lady Evelin's seeing the whole of my correspondence with you. Will she behold my attachment with unprejudiced eyes? She, perhaps, from her great partiality to me, may resent the ill treatment I sustained. But, perhaps," with a sigh still deeper, "the final period to his hopes, when he left England, joined to absence, may have effected a cure If so—But I need not anticipate "

I said all I could to prevent her harboring suspicions injurious to her peace, and the constancy of Darnley I repeated that part of Colonel Clayton's letter to you, which related to his companion I mentioned his sufferings "He has a susceptible heart," she said. "Sufferings! Yes, he did, he must have suffered" The silent tears stole down her cheek

Evelin-Abbey is a beautiful building I know your taste for Gothic structures As I was yesterday looking at it from an eminence in the park, the description of Harewood-Castle, in Mason's Elfrida, came into my mind

——————From its base
E'en to yon turret's trim, and taper spires,
All is of choicest masonry Each part
Doth boast a separate grace, but ornament,
Tho' here the richest that the eye can note,
Is us'd, not lavish'd, art seems generous here,
Yet not a prodigal

Well, but now will your Ladyship permit me to ask you how you approve of my conduct to Mr Mordaunt? Do you condemn my candidness?—I shall not be satisfied with myself, unless you tell me you think I acted right The honor your brother Lord Charles designed me, you know from the first, I declined I cannot help encouraging the idea, that my heart was destined to reward the constancy of Mordaunt On looking back, I think that is prettily expressed, a fine reward, truly!——I hope I shall ever think he has done me honor, and rewarded me above my deserts · but don't tell him I said so; yet, if you do not, he will find it out, for I mean to endeavor to convince him, for the future part of my life, that I think and know he has

A strange metamorphose this, you will think

Love,

Love, your Ladyſhip knows, has made many. And of this I am certain, I never felt that ſentiment for any man beſide. I loved his memory more than I cared to whiſper to myſelf; and as my knowledge of the world and my reaſon increaſed, my reverence, as I uſed to think it, increaſed likewiſe.

I have laid my heart before Caroline; ſhe expreſſes great ſatiſfaction; on a retroſpection I was almoſt tempted to repent of my plain dealing. I was afraid it had the appearance of offering myſelf to the acceptance of a man I had formerly rejected: but now I am convinced that true glory conſiſts in being capable of confeſſing and rectifying our faults: The firſt is always in our power, and I am not at all ſorry the laſt was. Is there any great merit in my adopting the above ſentiment? I fear not; ſince that alone will, in all probability, make me the happieſt of women. There is certainly ſome truth in the old adage, though it is ſeldom exemplified, that "Virtue is its own reward." This is aſſuredly the opinion of the world, which generally leaves it to its own reward.

Mr Mordaunt begged permiſſion to write to me; I forget whether I granted him leave or not; I hardly know what I ſaid; but I think I ſhould not be mortally offended with him, if he was to avail himſelf of my abſence.

Adieu! my dear Lady Betty,

Yours obediently,

SIDNEY VERE.

LETTER XCII

To Lady BETTY CRAUFORD.

Evelin-Abbey, June 15.

YEſterday Lady Evelin was reading to us, while we were employed with our needles. A ſer-

vant

vant entered, and delivered me a letter I opened it, not being well acquainted with the hand, I turned to the name "Good God! from Colonel Clayton"——"From Colonel Clayton!" repeated Caroline, with a tremulous voice. I read to myself There was a passage which made me shudder, it had a visible effect on my countenance, Caroline sat opposite to me, her work hanging in her hand,—her eyes rivetted on me "Ah! what is the matter?" asked she, in a tone softened by terror. "Nothing," answered I, in a low voice, "only he is in England." "In England! who is in England?—Is he come alone?"

To these interrogations I answered, "I believe so." The manner in which I expressed these words, alarmed Caroline She knew there was something I had concealed, and wished to conceal, from my not shewing her the letter "Then I am wretched," cried the dear girl, falling back in her chair "O Sidney! But tell me all"

"Be not thus alarmed, my love," hastening to her, and throwing the letter on an table by me, "Why these terrors?"

"What is the occasion of this, my dear Caroline? Dear Miss Vere what has thrown my child into this distress? May I not know the cause?"—I pointed to the letter Lady Evelin took it up "Will you permit me, Miss Vere?" "Most willingly, Madam"

Caroline sat, her hand supporting her head, the tears fast coursing down her pale cheeks.

"Here is nothing to alarm my child—The Colonel is well," said Lady Evelin, as she read, by which I found she thought he was the person for whom Caroline was most interested "But who," continued she, reading, "is this friend?" He say, "I wish I could have prevailed on my friend to accompany me home," "but he has taken the resolution

resolution of going to Corsica Though I know him brave, yet I fear he is more desirous of losing a painful existence, than of acquiring immortal glory, by defending the liberties of the exalted Paoli"———

"This is too much," exclaimed Caroline, faintly Her head dropped from her enervate arm, and she was sinking to the floor

I shrieked out, and endeavored to support her Lady Evelin was in agonies. "Speak, my beloved child! Ah, tell me, Miss Vere!" turning from one to the other, "What, O my God! am I to think?"

By this time the servants coming, gave every necessary assistance to my friend. She soon opened her eyes, looking round the room rather wildly; but instantly recovering her reason, and recollecting herself "Forgive me, my dearest madam—'Your pardon, too, my Sidney—But I cou'd not help it—Oh!—he is dead!—The last accounts from Corsica"—Tears gushed from her eyes—Her voice was stopped by sobs. Lady Evelin clasped her to her bosom, yet could give her no consolation, being ignorant of the true state of her daughter's heart, Caroline, from her extreme delicacy, being fearful of trusting her with its dearest secret

When the dear girl was a little composed, for I said every thing to dissipate her unnecessary fears, Lady Evelin said to her

"I have long, my dear, been desirous of knowing of some the incidents of your past life The accounts I have gathered have been imperfect. I find my child is not happy—Judge of my ready acquiescence to make you so, as far as in my power, by my earnestness to be acquainted with the particulars of your story The happiness within our reach I hope to procure you, tho' that is but small We cannot awake the dead,—or call our dear departed friend from the cold grave; but, if my endeavors

can

can facilitate any enjoyment for you on this earth, believe, you cannot be more ready to receive, than your fond mother be to confer."

"O, you are too good!—too kind, my indulgent parent! Why did I not open to you my whole heart before? But can I hope you will be partial to my follies, and participate in my distresses? Yes, I know you will; but I cannot be present. My dear Sidney has the letters which contain an account of my momentous life: from them you will learn what I have suffered. I bespeak your lenity. Permit me to retire, my dear madam."

"Do so, my best love."

I waited on Miss Evelin, as she now must be called, to her dressing-room. I staid but a moment with her, and returned to her Ladyship, whom I found involved in meditation. She rose when I entered. After some tender enquiries, she said, "I soon learned my daughter had a very susceptible heart, from whence I was surprized that she so heroically bore a disappointment, which the most amiable of men could not survive." Tears trickled down as she spoke; she, sighing, wiped them away, and proceeded. "Had Caroline loved as fervently as he did, as fervently as I am sure she is capable of loving, I had been bereaved indeed. I therefore conjectured some one had made a deeper impression on the heart of my child. Nothing transpired to give light to my surmises; and Caroline's carefully avoiding giving me any other than general accounts, silenced my enquiries. Why should she be reserved to her mother?"

"It proceeds alone, madam, from her extreme delicacy. Indulgent as she is to the failures of others, she is strictly rigid to herself; condemning that in her own conduct which generally receives commendation from the world."

"She has a thousand perfections."

"You

"You will say so, indeed, when you know her as I do. I will not delay you that satisfaction." I presented Lady Evelin with a box, wherein all Caroline's letters to me, and such of mine as could throw any light on her story, were contained. They were numbered in succession, to avoid any confusion. I then sought my friend.

I repeated what had passed. Caroline expressed her fears, which I represented as unreasonable and frivolous.

"They may be so," said she. "I have the best assurances from the indulgence of my mother,—but who, Sidney, can quiet my apprehensions for poor Darnley?——Ah! may he not at this instant be breathing his last? Oh! why did I not reveal this long attachment to my mother?"

"I cannot believe," returned I, "it would have made any alteration in your affairs; Sir George would still have been absent.—But surely, my dear, you are taking up sorrow at large interest. Why should you torment yourself with imaginary conjectures?"

"I read in St. James's Chronicle——"

"Which is not to be depended on always, Caroline. It is true, we have had an account of the total overthrow of the glorious Paoli, but, perhaps, that may be premature, if it be not, there is no certainty of Sir George Darnley's having reached Corsica; and if he has, why may he not have escaped, as well as the noble defender of his ancient liberties? Let us not, however, despond."

"Ah, Sidney! those ifs of your's may be fallacious."

"Your's, my love, are equally conjectural."

We spent some time thus together, when we were summoned to dinner. Every thing was ready. We waited some little time. Caroline asked if Lady Evelin had received notice. The servant answered

swered she had, but desired we would not wait for her, as she was too deeply engaged to think of eating. "Heavens!" said Caroline, "What am I to think? Perhaps my mother is displeased with me. Dearest Sidney! let us seek Lady Evelin. We found that tender parent weeping. "O! my dearest mother," said Caroline, approaching, and respectfully taking her hand, "Speak to me. Tell me, do you yet regard me as your faultless child? Ah! I fear not."

"My angel-daughter," wrapping her arms round Caroline, "I know not half my happiness. Yes, *I will look at you, and receive consolation*. But excuse me, my sweet girls, and dine without me." "I cannot leave you, my love, in this alarming situation."

"Where am I then, mamma?" asked my lovely friend, her eyes glistening with delight."

"In that odious house, after you left the Museum gardens."

"An alarming situation, indeed!" said I, "but as Caroline got very safely out of it, do, dear Lady Evelin, give us your company at dinner." She at length, by dint of persuasion, accompanied us.

"I see," said I, "my amiable Caroline has, by her eyes, asked your ladyship a question of importance several times."

"O! my Sidney."

"I guess what my dear girl's expressive eyes would ask. Let me but once see the man, and my instant concurrence shall convince you how much I approve your choice."

Caroline made suitable acknowledgments to her mother.

She learned from us, during dinner,—for we dispensed with the attendance of the servants,—many circumstances relative to Sir George Darnley. I favored Caroline's wishes, that her mother might be be prepossessed in his interest, as the subsequent part of his behavior to my amiable friend was reprehensible in some degree

I endeavored to convince Caroline, who seemed inslaved by her fears, that Miss Darnley would certainly take the earliest opportunity of apprizing her brother, with the change of affairs But lest she should not, I will request the favor of your ladyship, that you will dispatch an express to Colonel Clayton, and beg him under the strict seal of secrecy, as from himself, to apprize his friend with this late event Be the means of doing my beloved Caroline this service, and I shall be induced to forgive your ladyship for saying, "you think Mordaunt should have assumed the character I had laid aside, and fretted me a little, in order to inhance his merit with me" That is not like my sensible, amiably tender Lady Betty Craufurd—No; certainly some male creature imperceptibly seized your pen, and writing these lines, cast a mist before your eyes, lest when seeing you should erase them.

To punish you, I will tell you, Mordaunt writes better than you tho' he is incomprehensible sometimes—Indeed, he is much too precipitate A-propos! tell him, I will not think of marrying, till my friend is happy It that does not set you all to work to dispatch expresses, I do not know what will

I think the scheme you concerted with Colonel Clayton, to detect the wife of my father, a very feasible one But I second and applaud Mr Mordaunt's counsel against it——Of what advantage would the executing the warrant be?—I never can consent to the planting so sharp a dagger in the breast of my father He has used me hardly, and by her instigations—He may, most likely will, receive punishment enough thro' her.

The

The [illegible] consent that he has given to Mr Mordaunt's [illegible]wed addresses, I am afraid proceeds not s[illegible] from any remains of tenderness, as his desire— [illegible] ther, that which has been infused into him by my mother in-law of getting rid of me However, even that is acceptable, as without that a union could not for some time have taken place, and I could not have thought of encumbering Mr. Mordaunt, by giving him an indigent wife, and if my father had with-held his concurrence, he might likewise have with-held my fortune —Now, I think he must give up, what will be my own in a little more than a year, independent of him

I make no doubt but Mr Mordaunt's earnest solicitations for an early day proceeds from his great generosity, but we should not tax that noble sentiment too high

Adieu! my dear Lady Betty —I do not love you so well as I did, and yet you know not how dear you are to your

SIDNEY VERE.

LETTER XCIII.

To Lady BETTY CRAUFORD

Evelin Abbey, June 25

WE have got a venerable visiter here Mrs Grafton.

Lord L wrote a letter to that lady, confessing his villainy, and that of her infamous niece, which notwithstanding her artifices, he managed to have delivered into Mrs Grafton's own hand

The discovery of Caroline's innocence, gave her as much pleasure as the conviction of Letitia's baseness occasioned her sorrow About

At this time the amiable Caroline wrote to her patronefs, which fhe had refolved to do, when fhe had it in her power, to prove her innocence, and not before

An anfwer was immediately returned, filled with intreaties to be forgiven for her rafh judgment And that fhe was on the road to Evelin-Abby, as fhe could not reft 'till fhe had received pardon; and folded her darling to her heart, but had fent this notice by a meffenger, who was to bring a fpeedy anfwer, whether or not, her company would be acceptable

Caroline expreffed the utmoft impatience to fee her benefactrefs, as fhe heard fhe was but at the diftance of fifteen miles

Lady Evelin ordered the poft coach, and we all fet out for the inn, where we learned Mrs Grafton waited

The meeting between the venerable old lady, and the amiable and lovely young one, was very tender

Caroline in the moft graceful manner bent her knee to her patronefs, who haftily raifed and clafped her arms about her "O! my much injured child, can you pardon my cruel?"——

—"Ah! fay no more, my deareft, beft of friends —We were all deceived You acted from the beft, the jufteft principles Let us talk no more of what has paffed —Suffer me to introduce you to my much honored mother" Taking her hand, and prefenting her to Lady Evelin, who complimented her upon her great care of her daughter, &c Adding, "I have obligations to you, madam, of fuch a nature as I can never repay"

"Ah!" returned Mrs. Grafton, "all were cancelled by my injurious treatment How could I believe you guilty of crimes your foul abhorred? O my Caroline how much have I fuffered! I have never known one day of eafe fince your difgraceful difmiffion, dismission, notwithstanding, by the machinations of your enemies, I was fully convinced you merited the rigor with which you were treated. But thank God I am happy enough to be undeceived.—I have lived long enough."

On our return to the Abby, Mrs. Grafton told us, that tho' the treaty between Sir George Darnley and her niece was abrubtly broke off, yet she never knew the true reason, Miss Grafton having art enough to conceal it. To spare her niece the mortification of meeting Sir George in public, they retired into the country, where they continued till the receipt of Lord L—'s letter.—Miss Grafton was from home at the time. If Mrs. Grafton had wanted any corroborating circumstances, she found proofs enough in the vile Jenny, Miss Evelin's late servant, who had, for her faithful services, been retained about the person of her infamous employer.——

Mrs. Grafton was determined not to see her niece, therefore confined herself to her chamber, after having enclosed Lord L—'s letter in one, full of invective for her baseness, with strict injunctions to leave the castle immediately: her fixed resolve never more to behold her, and assurance, that she should lose the benefit of an annuity she meant to allow to enable her to live honestly, if she ever attempted to gain admission to her presence.

June 26.

A letter from Harriot Darnley! Sir George is arrived. The decisive blow was given to the Corsicans before his embarkation from Leghorn. Every thing must now fall out as we wish.

Caroline underwent a little perturbation, but I hope

hope more of the pleaſurable than painful.

Letters from all quarters All containing the utmoſt profeſſions of eſteem and intreaties for no longer remembering what is paſt, with congratulations by hundreds ——

Aye, it is all mighty well Caroline does not ſtand in need of their countenance to do her honor —The heireſs of eight thouſand a year, be ſhe what ſhe will, will not want worſhippers

She, ſweet, mild, forgiving creature, remembers only the former kindneſs her ineſtimable virtues exacted from them, while the whips and ſtings which patient merit of the unworthy takes, and the proud man's contumely, is totally driven from her memory I admire, I revere, but am afraid I could not emulate her.

As I live, Lady Evelin, with the moſt dignified delicacy, and truly polite freedom, has ſent an invitation to the Darnley family She wiſhes, ſhe ſays, to diſcharge her obligations to all her beloved Caroline's friends I am to come in for my ſhare, too, and how, Lady Betty, do you think that is to be effected? You cannot gueſs —Why, then, I will tell you She has intreated me, in her name, to requeſt the favour of a certain relation of your's company —I, ſmiling, told her ladyſhip "I could not do it"—"Then I will," ſaid ſhe And ſo it is to be, I think —But do not let him flatter himſelf, for I will adhere to my former reſolution of waiting till my friend is happy A formal invitation to the ſwain accompanies this. As I ſhall ſoon ſee him,—he won't want twice aſking, I hope.—I ſhall not anſwer his laſt letter

There is no need of making formal professions; I shall therefore say no more to you, or of him, than that I am both yours,

Sincerely,

SIDNEY VERE

LETTER XCIV.

To Lady BETTY CRAUFORD.

Evelin-Abbey, July 20

INDEED I believe I must fly to my dear Lady Betty for protection: Here, they are in a league against me. I am too weak to oppose them all, in vain have I deprecated the power of each in my favor A fine thing, indeed! that this man, this relation of yours, should carry all before him, and convert my friends,—friends of so long standing too, to my persecutors But I am afraid I should be as bad o, at Crauford-Manor: What, then, shall I do? Yield at discretion, they all say

I told your ladyship of all things being *en train* here But Caroline has requested from all her friends six months from the time of her amiable brother's decease I made the same reasonable request, but no, I am not to be indulged My words are wrested to *their* own meaning, and produced against me Is this using me well, Lady Betty? My asking you that question, puts me in mind of the drowning wretches catching at straws, for had you not shewn my letter to Mr Mordaunt, I should have been free from these hasty importunities On you, then, I must vent my spleen, as the primary cause.

I said.

I ſaid, "I would not think of marrying 'till I ſaw my friend happy that is, married, I ſay—But they put another conſtruction on my words They have, that is, Sir George and my hopeful intended, have tortured theſe poor words as never anagrammatiſt did, to make them of force againſt me But what vexes me moſt of all,—for your ladyſhip muſt know, I am greatly vexed, is, my ſweet Caroline gives me up How apt is indulgence to ſpoil even the moſt perfect—If her execution, as ſome witty perſon has phraſed it, depended on mine, I would be hanged if ſhe would not ſay a thouſand pretty and reaſonable things upon the ſubject I have a great deal on my mind to ſay, but what ſignifies throwing away one's eloquence on perſons who refuſe to hear the voice of the charmer.

I can better withſtand the united power of the whole junto, than the mild perſuaſive intreaties of my amiable Caroline I laugh at Mordaunt, bluſter at Darnley, reaſon with the ladies, turn Clayton out of the room, but ſilently attend to my friend I am predetermined, if they do ſucceed, ſhe alone ſhall have the merit of it Thoſe lords of the creation I abjure It is impoſſible to hold out always I ſuppoſe I muſt give up my favorite point of being married on the ſame day as Caroline.—But meekneſs like mine is always thus overpowered Caroline ſays ſhe is happy, ſo I muſt be fettered of courſe. "But ſuppoſe," you ſay, "you are not convinced ſhe is happy" Ah! my dear Lady Betty, do you think I have left any ſubterfuge untried? No it muſt be; but Caroline ſhall have the glory of the day. Apropos! Would it not be a political ſcheme, and in conformity to the ancient cuſtom of *Lex talionis*, when I have gained a powerful friend in Mordaunt, which my compliance alone can do, to join the confederates

againſt

against Caroline, and try the strength of her arguments against our abridging part of the requested six months?—A noble thought that! I shall improve it.

I told her to-day, it signified not talking, for I would not, with my own consent, marry 'till she did.

"My Sidney! my love!" returned she,—"whose happiness are you delaying! A Mordaunt's?—A man, whose constancy has gone thro' the severest trials.—A man, whose life has been for more than three years embittered.—I ask not by whom embittered. Ah Sidney! Do not by these unnecessary delays, recal to his wounded memory a period when my charming friend was not faultless."

"If I thought Mr. Mordaunt had the least doubt"——"My Sidney would not confirm those doubts, by still protracting the time of his happiness!—In your defence, which indeed my dear was a poor one, you have made happiness and matrimony synonimous terms. you said you would marry when you saw me happy, I am happy—I tell you so, and yet you refuse to fulfil your engagement."—

"Are you then happy Caroline?

"If happiness consists in having the wishes of our hearts gratified, I am happy Sidney. I wished to find my parents, I found the only one remaining. I wished my birth might be equal to the man I loved, it is—I wished to have the concurrence of all our mutual friends in our union,—that too is granted me—I wished to have my ruined fame cleared up to the world, that too is accomplished. I wished indeed."—Tears started in her eyes, sighs heaved her agitated bosom.

"O my Caroline!" throwing my arms round her neck, "you say you are happy.—Are these sighs and tears indications of happiness?

"Believe

"Believe me, my dearest Sidney, I am as happy as ever I can be—I am now at the summit of human felicity. But still, the sighing heart, in the midst of enjoyment, will sometimes remind us of human imperfection The tears I shed, must, while remembrance lasts, sometimes flow—Yet, my love, they are the tears of resignation"

"But why, my Caroline, may I not be indulged, without the imputation of making a man miserable, whom I wish to see happy? Why may we not change our names on the same day?"

"The cases, my dear, are widely different—I mourn the loss of an amiable unfortunate brother, whom I too lately discovered to be so I was to have been united to him Decency—reason, every thing is on my side, and only caprice, as the men call it, on your's—I would stile it delicacy, but not of the most genuine kind"

"You are not generous, Caroline, you join with men, against your poor friend"

"I cannot bear, my love, you should, even in jest, call me so I will no longer solicit you Mr Mordaunt shall owe your kind condescension to yourself His Sidney alone shall bless him"

"Forgive my petulance, my amiable Caroline Do with me as you will but let Mordaunt know it is to you he owes every thing praise-worthy in his Sidney"

"Amiable, charming girl, how I love you! you then allow me permission to pronounce to Mr. Mordaunt his happiness"

Thus this notable affair is settled, I suppose I have not been down stairs yet. I imagine I shall be pestered to death with their congratulations, and so forth. Well, it will soon be over.

Matrimony is an evergreen, always flourishing I have a *presentiment*, there is another couple have a mind to take a trip to the jubilee. I am much miſtaken if Harriot Darnley will not fall a ſacrifice to Clayton's attacks He has already opened an eye-battery againſt her, and they are full of combuſtible matter She makes but a weak defence, underſtands nothing of generalſhip.—Has no guard, and expoſes her undiſciplined forces to his veteran troops. They continue hoſtilities, but have not yet had a parly This is, I believe, a diſcovery, and I will further it all I can If they are ſo fond of matrimony, as to want to plunge men in it, they ſhall not remain long to laugh at me

---

July 21.

Well, I begin to think I have not done amiſs. I ſeem to receive an additional reſpect, now I am to commence matron ſo ſoon There is ſomething pleaſing in that attention from others, which ſeems to be our due, from the chearfulneſs with which it is paid

I don't like the being ſeparated from Caroline, but the affair muſt be concluded, it ſeems, at Crauford-Manor: unleſs my father ſhould inſiſt on the ceremony being performed, in the chapel at Vere-Park But that, I do not ſuppoſe, he will

I believe Mr. Mordaunt ſet the lawyers to work, as ſoon as he diſcovered my ſentiments. He tells me, the writings only want ſigning and ſealing to complete the buſineſs —

My dear Caroline has preſented me with a moſt elegant ſet of the fineſt pearls I ever ſaw Diamonds I have of my own, which, with the addition of Mr Mordaunt's family-jewels, will make me very ſplendid I hope, I ſhall ever poſſeſs the ineſtimable jewel, his heart, and the deuce take the reſt

On Monday next, Mordaunt, Clayton, and your obedient

obedient set out for your ladyship's habitation, and if nothing happens to prevent it, on Thursday, there will be an end to your devoted

SIDNEY VERE.

LETTER XCV.

To Sir GEORGE DARNLEY

Crauford Manor, July 30

YOU expect, you told me, a very circumstantial account of the wedding, &c which you are to communicate to the Ladies Are you aware, my dear Sir George, of the many difficulties which may accrue to your friend?—That while I am recounting one circumstance, I shall perhaps miss a thousand, altogether as important? But, to satisfy your demand, as well as I am able, yesterday was the day of days About ten, we were assembled in Lady Betty's dressing room As this letter is to be read to the ladies, I must not omit the article of the bride's dress—I am a wretched fellow at descriptions of this kind, I should shine infinitely superior, in describing fascines, batteries and bombardments

Miss Vere was dressed in a white gown, or negligée, I know not the different denominations of apparel, buttoned with pearls Her hair without powder, a pretty little cap, pearl-earrings and necklace, the same you saw at Evelin-Abbey Bracelets with pictures, the one, her destined husband, the other, her charming friend Altogether she looked inchantingly handsome She is, except two, the loveliest woman I know The first [illegible] exceptiors is Miſs Evelin, and the ſecond, I ſhall not yet name to you. Your Caroline, I think, far ſurpaſſes any of her ſex, but ſhe was made for love and Darnley. My heart felt many alarms on her account, but ſhe was from the firſt forbidden fruit. It was very near falling a victim to the little Sidney. When I firſt encountered her ſweet blue eyes, there were a couple of arch rogues of Cupids, with their bows bent, and taking full aim. "Not ſo faſt, my little friends," cried I, dropping my eyes a little lower, when I diſcovered another raſcal in a dimpled cheek.—But ſome obſtacles intervened, and I remained maſter of my heart, tho' its palpitations remained. While it was rather wavering between the two friends, like the holy Mahomet's tomb, comes a third, in the likeneſs of ——'Sdeath! I had like to have made a diſcovery; however, I believe, I am now fixed, and will, with your leave, reſume the thread of my diſcourſe, concerning the bride.

As ſoon as breakfaſt was ended, Mordaunt looked at his watch, the fair Sidney's face underwent the moſt pleaſing ſuffuſion.—She looked at Lady Betty, then on the carpet, then again on Lady Betty. Her amiable confuſion gave freſh beauties to her perſon. Mordaunt, with eyes beaming forth love, aroſe and approached, taking her hand. "Has my deareſt Sidney any objection? It is time, I believe." Her lips moved, but I could not hear what ſhe ſaid. On the inſtant the carriages drove up to the door, into the firſt ſtept Lady Betty, Miſs Vere, Mordaunt and I, the next was filled with Miſs Fitzroy, Miſs Lenox, Mr. Crauford, and Mr. Cleveland.

Sir William condeſcended to deſire his daughter would excuſe his not being preſent, for particular reaſons, I ſuppoſe: So this was all the *partie*.

The ceremony over,—which, by the bye, in ſome parts, is more ſolemn than I conceived it to be, be, We returned the married people in one coach, and the bride-men and maidens in the other We made a little excursion round the country, and came home by dinner time.

Mrs Mordaunt's behaviour the whole day was delicately charming, and ingenuously reserved, with the most modest chearfulness Her whole frame was animated

After dinner, in order *pour passer le tems*, a concert was performed, we all joining in the social harmony

Mordaunt intreated his fair wife to sing I had never heard her She took a book of Handel's oratoria songs, and accidentally turned to this song, and, with a voice softened to the utmost melody, sung —

> Would custom bid the melting fair
> The purpose of her soul declare,
> I then had call'd you mine,
> Long e'er the priest our hands had ty'd,
> And I became thy happy bride,
> At heaven's eternal shrine

Her husband, happy rogue, was all rapture. Every one joined in commendations of her performance She never appeared to such advantage as on that day, which proved a very agreeable one We danced cotillions, chatted pleasantly —In short, I liked the whole of it so well, that I should not repine if my time was come.

I am quite tired of batchelorizing any longer. —Do, dear Darnley, set me the example, and I will with pleasure follow it

I kiss the hands of all the ladies of Evelin-Abbey. Believe me to be

Yours sincerely,
HENRY CLAYTON.

LETTER XCVI.

To Miſs EVELIN.

Belfield-Lodge, Auguſt 30.

I AM extremely angry with Lady Wilton for robbing me of my lovely friend Why muſt ſhe carry you to the Grange? Do ſhorten your viſit as much as poſſible, and haſten to me I invite ye all Your Darnley muſt poſitively come.

So the little Harriot pouted, when you told her of my diſcovery: I am glad to hear you rallied her; firſt, becauſe ſhe deſerved it, for affecting to be diſpleaſed at an amiable ſenſibility; and, ſecondly, as it gave me a proof of your returning chearfulneſs

I got the ſecret out of Clayton preſently; but he looked a little confuſed, and begged I would not take notice of it, as he had not declared himſelf to Miſs Darnley.—I bade him then make haſte, for, to my certain knowledge, her heart was in imminent danger of deſerting its quarters.—I enjoyed his diſtreſsful curioſity extremely, but ſcorned to give up the dignity of my ſex on any account.

Mordaunt ſincerely wiſhes your requeſted ſix months were expired; ſo we all do Is not that a poſitive proof I have found nothing, in a whole month of matrimony, to repent of. If we go on at the rate we ſet out with, we ſhall be a moſt marvellous happy pair.

Your nuptials, my love, will enliven the gloomy month of November I could almoſt wiſh with the poet, "to annihilate both ſpace and time, and make two lovers happy."

To give pleaſure and happineſs is certainly the ſureſt way to enſure pleaſure and happineſs to ourſelves—I have found it ſo, ever ſince my connection with Mr. Mordaunt.—To tell you a ſecret, I am not

not at all ſorry I yielded to your ſolicitations, and thoſe of my dear Mordaunt I have never yet, nor do I think I ever ſhall, repent of giving *either* proofs of my tenderneſs

Adieu, my deareſt love. You and I have nothing left to wiſh for but a continuance of theſe bleſſings now in our poſſeſſion, or within our reach,

Yours faithfully,

SIDNEY MORDAUNT.

F I N I S.

Lightning Source UK Ltd.
Milton Keynes UK
UKHW050748010819
347174UK00004BA/132/P